Dann shows how Thoreau's free-ranging musings encompassed many of the otherworldly interests of his contemporaries, such as a fascination with faeries, mysterious appearances of gossamer, and other curiosities. Dann makes a strong case that while Thoreau's writings were grounded in tough-minded observations of nature, his own worldview and 'sympathetic science' were far from disenchanted."

—Fred Nadis, author of
The Man from Mars: Ray Palmer's Amazing Pulp Adventure
and *Wonder Shows: Performing Science, Magic,
and Religion in America*

"Far from the well-worn paths of academic scholarship, Dann acquaints his reader with a protagonist who is an American mystic, a new-age prophet, a cosmic explorer . . . Dann takes the road less traveled, leading a reader into out-of-the-way places, through hidden passages in Thoreau's personal life. . . . *Expect Great Things* is eccentric, strange, even far-fetched, but nonetheless admirable—a bit like Henry David Thoreau." —John Kaag, *The New York Times Book Review*

"In plumbing Thoreau's own singular and profoundly personal quest for the infinite, [Dann] delivers keen insights. A refreshing new perspective on an American icon." —*Booklist*, starred review

The Road to
WALDEN

The Road to
WALDEN

12 Life
Lessons from a Sojourn
to Thoreau's Cabin

KEVIN DANN

A TarcherPerigee Book

An imprint of Penguin Random House LLC
375 Hudson Street
New York, New York 10014

Most TarcherPerigee books are available at special quantity discounts for bulk
purchase for sales promotions, premiums, fund-raising, and educational needs.
Special books or book excerpts also can be created to fit specific needs. For
details, write: SpecialMarkets@penguinrandomhouse.com.

Library of Congress Cataloging-in-Publication Data
Names: Dann, Kevin T., 1956– author.
Title: The road to Walden : 12 life lessons from a sojourn to Thoreau's cabin /
Kevin Dann.
Description: New York: TarcherPerigee, [2018] |
Identifiers: LCCN 2017058109 (print) | LCCN 2018001071 (ebook) |
ISBN 9780525504719 | ISBN 9780143132837 (paperback)
Subjects: LCSH: Thoreau, Henry David, 1817–1862—Knowledge—Natural history. |
Thoreau, Henry David, 1817–1862—Influence. | Walking—Guidebooks. |
Self-realization. | BISAC: BODY, MIND & SPIRIT / Inspiration & Personal
Growth. | BODY, MIND & SPIRIT / Mysticism. | TRAVEL / Special
Interest / Literary.
Classification: LCC PS3057.N3 (ebook) | LCC PS3057.N3 D36 2018 (print) |
DDC 818/.309—dc23
LC record available at https://lccn.loc.gov/2017058109

Printed in the United States of America
1 3 5 7 9 10 8 6 4 2

BOOK DESIGN BY KATY RIEGEL

For my friends at Saint Francis House,

New London, CT

Contents

CHAPTER 1   Up Broadway: AWAKE!   1

CHAPTER 2   "When a Feller Needs a Friend": SPEAK!   23

CHAPTER 3   Learn to DANCE!   53

CHAPTER 4   Into the Vortex: CREATE!   75

CHAPTER 5   Captaining Huckleberry Parties: SENSE!   89

CHAPTER 6   Gone Fishin': SYMPATHIZE!   103

CHAPTER 7   Making Worlds: BEFRIEND!   113

CHAPTER 8   Fires Within and Without: BURN!   129

CHAPTER 9   In the Quiet Corner: BREATHE!   161

CHAPTER 10   The Respectable Folks: WHISPER!   171

CHAPTER 11   A Track Repairer in the Orbit of the Earth: LOSE!   185

CHAPTER 12   TRANSCEND!   195

APPENDIX   *12 Steps on the Transcendental Trail*   203

About the Author   205

"Lord, make me an instrument of your peace . . ."

Acknowledgments

IF NOT FOR THE ENTHUSIASM OF a single dedicated lover of Thoreau and of his students, Jeffrey Sinclair at Susan Wagner High School in Staten Island, and David Mahon, who asked if he could walk a while with me, I would not have taken the first step. Deep thanks to both of you. Thanks also to Joy Shaw, Gar Waterman, Walter and Phoebe Alexander, Maureen Curran, Bobby Matherne, and Paul Swanson for helping to put this pilgrim on the road. Margaret Carroll-Bergmann, director of Thoreau Farm, gave me a destination—and the sweetest invitation to sing I have ever received.

I am grateful for the wit, wisdom, and whimsy of dear friends: Jeff Prant, Ian Clyne, Jim Wetmore, Robert Powell, Lacquanna Paul, Len Raymond, Grace Panko, and Cathline Marshall. Thanks to Mitch Horowitz for inviting me out of bounds.

The pilgrim at each step lives on the kindness of strangers, whose acts of hospitality transform them into friends. Thanks to Mazen and to all those who came out to celebrate the Captain of a Huckleberry Party along the road to Walden; to Madhu Gupta, Michele Van Epps, Julie Menders, Margaret Morrissey, and your helpful public library staffs; and to all those who gave comfort, conversation, and compassion along the way.

Preface

"Thoreau Believed in Fairies" proclaimed the January 13, 2017, *Wall Street Journal* headline for the review of *Expect Great Things*, my biography of Henry David Thoreau. Though not quite as scornful as a 2016 *New Yorker* essay about Thoreau entitled "Pond Scum," that *WSJ* headline suggested that the sage of Concord might not get a fair hearing in New York City, even in his bicentennial year. Perennially misunderstood since his death at age forty-four in 1862, Thoreau had a tough time getting a fair hearing even in his own lifetime. In his eulogy for Thoreau, Ralph Waldo Emerson lamented that "instead of engineering for all America, he was the captain of a huckleberry party." Despite his affection for his protégé, Emerson was put off by Henry's wild ways; subsequent generations have embraced Thoreau's quests for outer wildness, while slighting his paramount fidelity to *inner* wildness. His carefully cultivated inner wildness is what made Henry both happy Captain of

Huckleberry Parties and ardent abolitionist content to go to jail rather than pay a poll tax in support of slavery.

In 2017, two hundred years after Thoreau's birth, it struck me that America could use a few more huckleberry parties, impromptu gatherings where a circle of neighbors—some strangers to one another—might amble out in search of sun-ripened sweet fruit, singing songs and reciting poetry. Rather than organize a book tour, I thought that the best way to honor my boyhood hero in his bicentennial year would be to christen myself "Captain of a Huckleberry Party," commit Henry's favorite song and a few of his poems to memory, and, traveling light—my down bag and battered inflatable sleeping pad the main necessities in my thirty-year-old frameless climbing pack—set out on a celebratory twelve-day walking pilgrimage from my birthplace—Manhattan—to his—Concord, Massachusetts. Those 235 miles traversed no barren Cape Cod dunes nor deep Maine spruce forests, but dozens of suburban New England communities whose character and history might be counted upon to yield insights about what America has become since Thoreau's time.

Henry Thoreau loved to hyphenate the word "extra-vagant" in order to transform its meaning from "outrageous luxury" to "walking beyond boundaries"—the core of his personal practice of both living and walking. Walking to Fitchburg, to Cambridge, across Cape Cod, or to the top of Mount Katahdin, Thoreau ever and always confronted both the wild places without and the wilder and more mysterious places within. The acuteness of his outer observations was always matched by the intensity of his inner soul-stretching, his relentless examination of himself in relation to the world. Inner examination wed to inner wildness is what makes Thoreau's masterpiece—*Walden*— as much a tale of pilgrimage as his more "vagrant" books: *A Week on the Concord and Merrimack Rivers, Cape Cod, The Maine Woods*, and his posthumously published "Walking" essay. America's first and still foremost indigenous sacred text, *Walden* is truly an antidote to our relentless national tendency to follow the broad way of stasis, complacency, and materialist comfort. Its every sentence challenges us to walk the narrow way, out of bounds and into a life of goodness, truth, and beauty.

Walden is a tour de force of aphoristic philosophical expression, and on my pilgrimage to Walden, I daily found myself reflecting—as both a meditative focus and an invitation to action—upon its philosophy of curiosity, attention, and liberation. Walking up Broadway, or a thousand other American broad ways, at each step one has the potential to capitulate, to stay asleep, to surrender, or to practice extra-vagance, to commit to wakefulness, wisdom, and wildness of heart and mind and deed. Though I took twelve days to reach Concord on April Fool's Day of 2017, I'd had a long lifetime of steps that helped me to appreciate *Walden*'s wisdom, as well as to recognize its blind spots, its limitations, its *bounds*. We live in a very different world from Henry's antebellum America, so that the eternal truths he explored have become only more exacting as guideposts for the good life. Walking to Walden with the intention to both celebrate Henry Thoreau and embody his ideals, I discovered just how challenging that path continues to be.

CHAPTER 1

Up Broadway: AWAKE!

Surely Henry David Thoreau was the most incongruous pedestrian who ever trod lower Broadway. In the fall of 1843, Thoreau had come to Staten Island to serve as tutor to the children of Ralph Waldo Emerson's brother William. He was still a year and a half away from his radical remove from Concord Village out to his homely cabin on the south shore of Walden Pond, yet he had plenty of contrarian critique of this world-renowned avenue of luxury. At P. T. Barnum's American Museum, which faced both St. Paul's Chapel and America's premier luxury hotel, the Astor House, Thoreau was treated to a kind of proto-Disneyland, a spectacular simulacrum of adolescent American fantasies of exoticism, cheap titillation, and vicarious adventure. Writing to Ralph Waldo Emerson but a week or two after his arrival, Thoreau described a cartoon canoe race on the Hudson between "Chippeway" Indians and straw-boater-topped Gothamites. The farce was almost as foolish as the "buffalo hunt" Barnum staged across the river in Hoboken. The showman's "free" spectacles (Barnum was collecting a considerable cut of the ferry fares) were the real sideshows, thought Thoreau: "Canoes and buffaloes are lost, as is everything here, in the mob." Encountering hordes of immigrants going up Broadway from Castle Garden, whole families cooking their dinner on the pavements, Concord's vagrant philosopher had hoped that they might preserve their individuality in this New World: "It must have a very bad influence to see so many human beings at once—mere herds of men."

On the first day of the spring of 2017, padding that same pavement in my well-worn walking shoes, it was hard not to weep bitter tears over Henry's nearly two-century-old lament. In the place of hoe-toting Norwegians and sunburned Irish and Italians there were clustered around the voluptuous bronze *Charging Bull* adjacent to Broadway's Bowling Green hundreds of selfie-snapping tourists, jockeying round its Taurean testicles at one end, its flaming vampire squid Wall Street nostrils at the other. A thousand portraits an hour uploaded to Instagram and Facebook and WeChat might serve as symbol as well as any other contemporary symptoms of a profound and troubling somnambulism at Broadway's foot and across America and the whole world.

That antebellum autumn on Staten Island, Thoreau was himself suffering from an acute episode of somnambulism; his sleep was literally interrupted by the "family curse" of sleeplessness. For the wide-awake Thoreau, it merely doubled his resolve to rise alert and aware, and to champion to his neighbors the benefits of being wide awake. Of all Henry's "excur-sions"—in that classic sense of deviating from a direct course—in those years leading up to his two-year Walden Pond experiment in living, the New York City sojourn most directly inspired his embrace of his most famous mantra: *Simplify. Simplify.* SoHo's spring 2017 shop windows have nothing on A. T. Stewart's Marble Palace, a block north of City Hall, and a long line of luxury-laden Broadway arcade windows in autumn 1843. Just blocks off Broadway, Henry's pavement-pounding manuscript peddling had finally found its mark, with John L. O'Sullivan, who published Thoreau's essay "Paradise (To Be) Regained" in his *United States Magazine and Democratic Review.* The piece was more than a savaging of J. A. Etzler's 1842 technotopian book *The Paradise within the Reach of All Men, without Labor, by Powers of Nature and Machinery*; it was a prophetic plea for America to bring an inner "motive power" equal to its outer one: "There is a certain divine energy in every man, but spar-ingly employed as yet, which may be called the crank within— the crank after all,—the prime mover in all machinery—quite indispensable to all work. Would that we might get our hands on its handle!"

Today that sublime and secret handle seems more elusive than ever. The "crank" of nearly all human endeavor reduced to the tip of one's index finger, the arcade window shrunk now to the size of an index card, we universally worship at the altar of menu consciousness, our relentless expectation of Heaven on Earth now supremely satisfied by the hidden magic of the sili-con chip behind a slick glass screen. It is perhaps too obvious to point out that we have fallen far from the $28.12½ cents' worth of boards, lath, old brick, casks of lime, iron nails, hinges, and screws of Henry's Walden cabin, or the $8.7½ cents he spent for provisions he consumed (all else he raised himself) in his two-year residence at the pond. We all sense that we are awash in a tide of luxury, an ersatz "Paradise" that makes Hurricane Sandy's storm surge seem trifling. America is drowning in its own prodigious prodigality, inundated by "Broadway," estranged from Walden Pond, and *Walden*.

ℬ

THROUGHOUT THE SUMMER AND FALL of 2017 the Cathedral of Commerce—the Woolworth Building—was wearing a black shroud upon her crown, as her upper floors were converted from office space to luxury apartments. Alchemy Properties hired Thierry Despont, the architect who oversaw the conversion of the Ritz Paris, for the job. While one-bedrooms can be had for as little as $4.5 million, and whole-floor spreads for $26.5 million, the seven-story penthouse will run you $110 million or so. Even F. W. Woolworth, the five-and-dime department store magnate who built this tallest-in-the-world office tower in 1913 with cold cash, would not be able to come up with that kind of money.

From the glorious Gothic entrance and from the east-facing windows of every one of those new palatial apartments, as one looks just slightly north to City Hall, one sees Manhattan's most understated monument to the American Revolution. The top of the City Hall flagpole is crowned with a gold weather vane bearing the simple word LIBERTY. It is no vague slogan, but a faithful remembrance of the Liberty Poles erected upon this once-English common, where King George III's soldiers were quartered in barracks that stood just about where the Tweed Courthouse stands today.

In my mind's eye, I always see a gang of red-capped Gotham teenagers raising those stolen British navy masts in the middle of the night, silently counting coup against the Crown with the scarlet LIBERTY flag that flew from its spire. I imagine most of those Liberty Boys as seventeen—my age when I read *Walden* for the first time. Passing it on this March 20, I am reminded that it was March 21, 1769, when the British army chopped the Liberty Pole down after that month's Stamp Act repeal celebrations. The next time the Liberty Boys put up a pole on the common, they sheathed it in iron to stop the British soldiers' axes; the commemorative flagpole is similarly sheathed.

Though you can't now see the spot from Broadway's sidewalk, it was just two blocks from here that the "First Blood" of the American Revolution was spilled, six weeks before the Boston Massacre. Redcoats attacked a group of citizens defending the Liberty Pole raised in the Golden Hill wheat field—about where the John Street Church stands today. Francis Field, an innocent bystander, was slashed in the face by a British bayonet as he stepped out to see what the ruckus was. A peddler and fisherman were injured, and another man took a near-fatal bayonet stab in his chest.

F. W. Woolworth might rightly say that New York City, and America with it, has nickled-and-dimed its way from the courageous spirit of the Sons of Liberty to our current cowardly, craven posture of luxury. Our national obsession with luxury stands starkly caricatured before all the world in the person of one of Gotham's native sons, whom American citizens freely placed in the highest office of the land. That the nation's first president humbly walked from Federal Hall on Wall Street, up Broadway to a service at St. Paul's Chapel—a block south of the Woolworth Building—after his inauguration goes unremembered and uncelebrated, while ten thousand tourists a day stream under the golden threshold of this or that Trump Tower, sleepwalking to the deadly drumbeat of the American cult of celebrity.

Born a stone's throw from where the "shot heard round the world" was fired, Henry Thoreau never for a moment forgot that the price of liberty was eternal vigilance. Only five years before his birth, Concord's citizens, including his father, had fought a second war for independence against that empire of luxury—Great Britain. Those who had taken part in the events had tutored Henry and other Concord children in tales of the Revolution. He heard from his mother's mother that after her Tory brothers had been arrested, she had smuggled metal files to them in the Concord jail. An elderly neighbor told Thoreau how her brother, the morning after the famous battle, had come home to fetch cider and cheese for himself and his fellow Minutemen. That the Battles of Lexington and Concord were known by all Thoreau's neighbors as simply the "Concord Fight" attests to the degree to which this mythic event was engraved into both the local landscape and the folk soul. That he began his Walden Pond vigil on the Fourth of July was the simplest and most obvious of his often obscure choices.

Manhattan's role as American cultural capital tends to erase

local myth and legend in favor of the national. The sidewalk of
lower Broadway is punctuated with 206 granite flagstones commemorating ticker-tape parades from the Battery to City Hall
Park. In the wake of the first ticker-tape parade celebrating returning World War I soldiers, the ritual quickly devolved into
imperial posturing, from the 1924 parade for the American
Olympic team to Charles Lindbergh's triumphal transatlantic
flight in 1927, and then, from 1945 to 1965, 130 parades to welcome foreign heads of state. In 1969, John Lindsay threw a parade for the Mets! The city's "Canyon of Heroes" conveniently
obliterates Broadway's august history of rambunctious street
rebellions—beginning with the July 9, 1776, parade from the
Commons down to Bowling Green to tear down the gilt eques-
trian statue of King George III after the first public reading in
New York of the Declaration of Independence. Such truly heroic local events are in danger of disappearing completely from
living memory. It is sobering to think that as recently as 1899,
New York City's most celebrated monument was the flagpole at
Battery Park, up which John van Arsdale—who had enlisted as
a sailor at age nineteen—had shimmied on the twenty-fifth of
November 1783, to replace the Union Jack with the American
flag. As General George Washington and his troops paraded
down Broadway, the street filled with New Yorkers celebrating
the end of seven years of British occupation.

"Luxury," "extravagance," "false refinements" were the by-
words of Revolutionary rhetoric, linked inextricably to British
tyranny. Even as the Woolworth Building was raised up on
Broadway, to a man its builders—masons, carpenters, steel-
workers, and sculptors—knew the tale of John van Arsdale and

the Battery Park flagpole. Stand on the sidewalk today, at quitting time on any weekday afternoon, and ask the guys with hard hats what New York's most heartily celebrated holiday was for the first century after American independence. Not a soul can answer Evacuation Day—November 25. But most will freely guess how much Donald Trump is worth.

℃

MY NOTION—like Henry's—was to walk deliberately, to "front only the essential facts of life" as I headed out toward Concord, and so my goal on that first day of spring was to lay my head down on the earth inside one of the Indian caves up in Inwood Hill Park that evening. Having walked and bicycled Broadway's length dozens of times, I had no doubt I'd reach my destination by midafternoon, immune to any of Broadway's delicious distractions. Union Square, Madison Square, Herald Square, Times Square, Columbus Circle—not one of the eccentric agoras kept me from my steadfast allegiance to walk upstream, to feel the invisible rush of energy that comes when one walks north against the southward-streaming traffic. Though the prevailing wind on Mannahatta is from the south, any wide-awake body takes immediate note of a more palpable current from the north, a track laid down in the ether by ten thousand years of moccasined feet and a couple of centuries of pedestrians, peddlers' carts, streetcars, and automobiles. Like walking or running in the woods when the trees press close along the path, that current imparts vigor and vitality, an electricity wholly hygienic in contrast to the neon and LCD emanations of Times and other Broadway squares.

I pass a thousand moments of my own biography as I walk north, each one bringing a small pulse of gratitude for the deep mystery that is life. And then, up at 166th Street, I am stopped dead in my tracks. NewYork-Presbyterian/Columbia University Medical Center is a massive, beige brick, postwar building— really four buildings all on top of one another. Somewhere up among those anonymous windows, on March 25, 1956, I was born. I wondered how my mother could have abided such a monstrous edifice as the place to welcome her firstborn. In the space of sixty seconds, three different emergency vehicles screamed up to the hospital's entrance. I retreated across Broadway to a little green sanctuary called Mitchell Square.

A thin sliver of land wedged between Broadway's wide swath and St. Nicholas Avenue, with only a half dozen benches and no other amenities, this park seems more orphaned than my imagination of all the babies born across the street. There is only a single London plane tree, half a dozen Callery pears, and a misshapen locust at its northern end where the park comes to a narrow point. A glacially smoothed bit of bedrock, big enough for a ball team to sit on, crops out right smack-dab in the center of the park. I stepped up to this humble summit of schist, faced south toward the sun, closed my eyes, and recalled words spoken by Joan of Arc, as she confronted her difficult destiny six centuries ago.

"I was born to do this. May God keep me here. I act, so that God will act." I've long forgotten where I first heard Joan's

three-part prayer and pledge; most likely it was from Mark
Twain's *Personal Recollections of Joan of Arc*, his 1896 serial-
ized novel, which he had published anonymously in order to
free his readers from hearing it in his renowned comic satirical
voice. There seemed in Twain's relationship to Joan something
of the singularity of destiny that marked her extraordinary life.
One day in 1849, while the thirteen-year-old Sam Clemens was
working as a printer's devil (an apprentice who performed a
number of tasks) in Hannibal, Missouri, a gust of wind blew a
stray leaf from a book across his path. Picking it up, he discovered that it described the persecution in prison by rough English soldiers of a person called "Joan of Arc"; on this single
page he read the story of how the soldiers had stolen her clothes.
Sam hurried home and asked his mother and older brother if
Joan of Arc was a real person, and learned that she had been a
young French peasant girl who had saved her nation from English tyranny. He would on occasion describe this story as the
turning point of his life; indeed, from the moment of finding
that tumbling page on that Hannibal street, the worlds of both
history and literature opened up to young Samuel Clemens,
and, though history has largely neutralized his radicalism, he
became a fiery crusader for justice. Twain seemed to be drawn
to Joan's story because he saw it as the epitome of the age-old
struggle of the common folk against political and religious op-
pression by those more powerful. Twain's story of Joan of Arc
affirmed the value of a spiritual life at a moment when his culture was madly pursuing a path of industrialism, imperialism,
and materialism.

Joan had not always been so celebrated. She was reviled by

William Shakespeare in the sixteenth century; neglected in the seventeenth; ridiculed by Voltaire in the eighteenth. It is perhaps unsurprising that critics panned Twain's book; he considered it his best, while they called it his worst. Urbane, naturalistic, "scientific" America was not ready for La Pucelle—a wisp of a girl who was given sword and shield by fairies, and armor and armies by the French king. That such a boundary-crosser as Joan should have found her champion in that cussed Clemens was no coincidence. It was as natural as Henry Thoreau's fondness for the abolitionist John Brown. They were one wild pack of rule-breakers and truth-tellers, the nightmare of all empire, privilege, and falsehood.

"I was born to do this." Thoreau echoed Joan's commitment in his *Journal* declaration that "I have never got over my surprise that I should have been born into the most estimable place in the world; and in the nick of time, too." Can you imagine how fully the world would be transformed if this confidence in one's own destiny were a universal birthright, a pedestal for personal action in the world? One hallmark of the hero is that he or she has one particular story to tell of his or her own awakening, and then tells it over and over. Joan in her brief life spoke often and with great reverence of how Saint Michael and Saint Catherine had come to her below the hawthorn tree in her father's Domrémy garden when she was but thirteen—the same age as young Sam Clemens when he came upon her tale. Henry Thoreau was just twenty when Ralph Waldo Emerson, with a single question—"What are you doing now? Do you keep a journal?"—gave Thoreau his life's work.

My own adolescent awakening, an unmistakable epiphany

that set its stamp upon my life, came at age seventeen. One Saturday evening in the summer of my junior year in high school, my parents had left me to look after my younger sister Melissa while they were out to a party. On any sultry summer night my absolute favorite thing in the world to do was to sail down Main Street of my New Jersey village on my ten-speed, arms up in the air, even as the bike bumped over the railroad tracks at the center of town. I suspect I was singing out some wild Springsteen anthem as I went. Melissa was thirteen, old enough to be on her own, and so I slipped out for a ride . . . only to wake the next morning on a cot in the rec room of the Lutheran minister Pastor Creadick—the father of my best friend Peter, who had hailed me from the lawn of the high school as I passed on my bike. A few bottles of Boone's Farm later, according to Pete's account, he was trying to stuff me into a fifty-five-gallon drum out back by the auto shop in order to hide me from the cops, who had been called to break up our loud drinking party. He said that every time he put the lid on the drum, I would burst up and out, shouting: "I'm going to save the world! I'm going to save the world!"

I have told that story over and over, to my daughter, my friends, strangers, always as a kind of oafish admission that a pronounced missionary streak runs through my biography. To be a missionary, one must feel one has been given a mission, and that inebriated seventeen-year-old hopping out of the drum was giving voice to something that someone had whispered in his ear. When and where and who whispered are lost to my memory, but the gravity at the heart of that teenage misdemeanor has never escaped me. I was indeed born to do something for the world, and though it might elude me for decades, I was going to stick to my story.

Study Henry's life just a little, and you will soon see that his youth was marked by the same sort of missteps and misdemeanors—he once nearly burned down the Concord woods! *Your* youth, of course, has but variations on this eternal theme, and you would do well to do the same as Henry and Joan and Mark Twain and even me: find your story, soon, and stick to it. As Henry put it: *Know your own bone. Gnaw on it, and gnaw it still.*

Henry and I shared uncommon good fortune; ours was no difficult destiny. Still, *every* birth is a hero's birth, every incarnation potentially the inauguration of a hero's journey. Henry had been my hero, fated to me as surely as Henry had been to Thor and Sir Walter Raleigh, or Mark Twain to Joan of Arc. "Every man," said Thoreau in *Walden*, "is the builder of a temple, called his body, to the god he worships, after a style purely his own . . . We are all sculptors and painters, and our material is our own flesh and blood and bones."

Just a half hour's walk north from Mitchell Square, Broadway makes its most dramatic turn, bending east away from the rocky ramparts of the Fort Tryon ridge. There at that bend I found it most difficult to stick to my path, for atop that ridge stands Manhattan's most breathtaking assemblage of holy heroes—the Cloisters. It suddenly struck me that a visit to the Cloisters—the quietest, most Walden-esque temple on this noisy, Mammon-esque isle—would please Henry immensely, so off Broadway I went, up along the park's terraced pathways to John D. Rockefeller Jr.'s masterpiece of medieval-meets-modern architecture. As I stepped into the Late Gothic Hall, the first treasure to catch my eye—a fifteenth century Palmesel, or "palm donkey," an intricately carved red-robed Christ astride a donkey,

all atop a rude wooden-wheeled cart—seemed the perfect welcome for an anachronistic Walden-bound pedestrian. Immediately to the left was a half-sized sculptural assemblage of the
Three Kings attending the infant Jesus; to the right, a full-sized
Archangel Michael with his foot on the neck of the dragon, hovering above the whole hall. The polished oak of Michael's
breastplate shone like actual steel armor, and the sculpted
wooden monster seemed alive. How Henry would have loved
this juxtaposition of martial valor and rude humility!

In the great room displaying the famous *Unicorn Tapestries*,
I was sure that Henry's attention would immediately center on
the narwhal tusk next to the hall's great hearth. He would love
its alabaster purity—emblem of the very quality he cultivated at
Walden Pond.

In the hall holding the *Nine Heroes* tapestries, I passed the
Hebrew heroes—Joshua, David, Judas Maccabeus; then the
pagan heroes—Hector, Alexander the Great, and Julius Caesar;
and finally the Christian heroes—Arthur, Godfrey of Bouil-
lon, and Charlemagne. Henry was more classicist than medie-
valist, but he would have loved every nook and cranny of the
Cloisters. While Emerson was off lecturing in Europe, and had
the chance to visit Chartres and Notre-Dame and other cathe-
drals, Henry had stayed in Concord, tending Waldo's garden,
filling his wood box, cleaning out the well. He had never seen a
Gothic cathedral, never heard the bells from the Tower of London, never walked the streets of Florence and Paris and Rome,
as had his dear friend. The Maine and Minnesota woods were
the most remote corners of his vagabondage, and Broadway
surely the most exotic.

for the point of land now known as Battery Park—at the south, plucked and polished by the great glacier that passed through here twelve thousand years ago. Nowhere is the plucking and polishing more apparent than in Inwood Hill Park, and nowhere on the big island can one more easily imagine Manhattan's aboriginal past. At exactly the same moment as the city's first skyscrapers were rising from the bedrock down on lower Broadway, amateur archaeologists like Reginald Pelham Bolton and William Louis Calver were digging toward the bedrock here for the remains of the island's first inhabitants. One of the first places they dug was my intended campsite for the night— the "Indian caves" in the Clove, the lovely little tulip poplar and hickory ravine spilling down toward the Spuyten Duyvil Creek.

Leaving Broadway at Isham Street—whose corner is marked by the Church of the Good Shepherd, founded by Paulist fathers in 1911 for the local Irish Catholic community and where Capuchin Franciscan friars now minister—I made a beeline for the Clove. Most of the day had been cold and damp, and I was keen to see whether the earth was dry inside the caves. None of the tulip trees were yet sporting any chartreuse; only a few young hickory buds were about to break open. I wished the season were a little further along, for just up the ravine a little was a broad, gentle hillside that would be carpeted with Dutchman's-breeches by mid-April, as the spicebush above them leafed out. Seven years ago, in the wake of a wicked nor'easter that swept along this ridge, toppling the tallest tulip trees, a lovely Japanese man had made beautiful wild sculptures out of the fallen branches and stumps. All that spring he could be seen there, where a bubbling spring came up in sand jets near the broken macadam path. He fed chickadees and nuthatches from his hand; the whole place was like Saint Francis's hermitage at Mount Subasio—or Henry's at Walden Pond, for he too ministered to the wild animals.

Before going to check on the Dutchman's-breeches and bubbling spring, I climbed the narrow path up to the caves. Along with the woodpeckers and white-throated sparrows, I heard some strange noise—like a radio. It was coming from the largest of the cave openings. There were Chicken of the Sea tuna cans and plastic gallon water jugs scattered about among the leaf litter—somebody feeding wild cats, I thought.

A bed of black plastic bags lined the floor of the cave, and there were more plastic jugs and other refuse lying about. A pair of boots, and . . . a tabby cat, her paws tucked in modestly, looking out at me. Then, as I stepped forward to say hello, the ground beneath her moved and a large man turned slightly in his cave bed, causing the tabby to also shift her position. The radio seemed to be tuned to a local AM station. Not wishing to disturb the cave dweller any further, I scampered down the slope a ways, then scouted out the other openings in the hillside. There was one place just barely long enough to fit my sleeping pad and bag, and its dry brown dirt floor sloped perfectly to elevate my head a little.

❧

A CAVE DWELLER now too, when I awoke the next morning, Tuesday the twenty-first, I heard the caveman's radio before the chickadees and nuthatches. The big fellow was up and about already, so I sauntered across to say good morning.

Pointing over the Spuyten Duyvil marsh toward the rising sun, Sabas—a Korean War veteran with a shaggy white beard who took his name from Saint Sabas, a fifth century monk who lived to almost one hundred in a Judean desert cave—extolled the virtues of the morning. "Just to wake and watch the sun come up, just to live. It's great, isn't it?" Later I would learn that Sabas sometimes puts into the Hudson at the foot of Dyckman Street and then floats upriver on the rising tide right into that marsh, using a watermelon as a buoy.

"Morning is when I am awake, and there is a dawn in me," Henry says in Chapter Two of *Walden*. But the book really opens—*wakes*—with Thoreau singing the praises of the morning, and of awakeness. These crystal-clear paeans to dawn alternate with Thoreauvian hide-and-seek, or, more exactly, hide-in-plain-sight playfulness:

* "If I should attempt to tell how I have desired to spend my life in years past, it would probably surprise those of my readers who are somewhat acquainted with its actual history; it would certainly astonish those who know nothing about it."
* "I will only hint at some of the enterprises which I have cherished."
* "You will pardon some obscurities, for there are more secrets in my trade than in most men's, and yet not voluntarily kept, but inseparable from its very nature."

✱ "I would gladly tell what I know about it, and never paint
'No Admittance' on my gate."

And yet, this welcome gesture, this declaration of open admission, itself conceals a secret, just as every cave opening only
hints at the darkness, the obscurities, within. Henry's promise
concealed a more sacred promise, one I share, and yet would
now go beyond, if only to confess that when I awake, I feel that
I have slept with angels.

All spiritual experiences are like gossamer, that spidery stuff
that on certain halcyon days in some years descended on the
Assabet River, and which was gone before Henry could fetch it
from the bottom of his skiff. Gossamer stuff shrinks and van-
ishes in the harsh light of day, when the world has woken up.

One must catch it at dawn or at dusk, when the light is low
and voices are muted. Henry knew this as well as any mortal,
and he carefully preserved the sanctity of his "auroral" hours.
Leaning in to his journal, he chronicled dreams and visions and
voices that came unbidden, but with a force as titanic as the gossamer was ephemeral.

Angels do not shout. They do not gesticulate or insist. They
whisper and are gone, leaving you, their friend, to lean in, to
work through, to know and gnaw. They are nothing if not faithful, and though deaf and blind and dumb you may be to their
subtle promptings, they will find every opportunity to whisper and wink at you again. The best preparation for recognizing
their arrival is to do nothing more than the task that Emerson
set for Henry: "Do you keep a journal?"

Put that cell phone in a drawer, or at the bottom of a closet.

Meditate into your journal. Write poems into your journal. Draw into your journal. *Awake* into your journal, and then into your own life. There are angels waiting for you to do this, and your every conscious act of wakefulness will draw them closer, so that you can hear them more clearly, as they help you see just which step lies ahead, crafted particularly for *you*. I could not tell you the story of that echo in the Saint-Guilhem Cloister, unless I had entered the courtyard in a condition of expectation, nor if I had not quickly written it down somewhere. Guilhem's quiet call; the Joan story from some nineteenth century primer, tumbling like a tumbleweed across Mark Twain's path; Henry's chance meeting with Emerson on Main Street; these things are mercurial, easily overlooked, sleepwalked through. Don't sleep through what the angels have brought you. AWAKE!

#1: AWAKE! And know that you have slept with Angels.

CHAPTER 2

"When a Feller Needs a Friend": SPEAK!

TORTURE

I know my piece before I speak—I've studied it for one whole
  week.
But when I stand before th' school I get to feelin' like a fool, An'
  ever'thing is jumbled so
It's worse than if I didn't know. I bet you old De-mos-the-nes
He never went to schools like these!   —CLARE BRIGGS (1914)

WALKING THE KINGS Highway from Pelham into New
Rochelle, New York, one is greeted by the most wonderful sign:

The Place to Come

NEW ROCHELLE

When a Feller Needs a Friend

On the top of this hospitable legend there strides a robust
young lad flanked by a trio of lovable mutts. In an instant
one can see that the Feller is the kind of boy you'd like to

have around—by nature gregarious, and one who travels for the most part in gangs. He is freckled and feckless, first cousin to Tom Sawyer and Huck Finn. He of course goes about with dogs—a whole pack of them. The Feller walks out of bounds by nature; no ruffled collars or starched shirts for this boy! He plays marbles for keeps, and gets a black eye now and again. He might smoke a butt behind the woodshed, and hates practicing on the parlor piano. A bit too twentieth century and irreverent to pass for a twelve-year-old Henry Thoreau; still, Henry would like this boy. Indeed, Henry and I both seem to think he is *exactly* the boy to whom we are speaking when we take our walk together, or sit in front of our own cabin.

Like the other signs that mark the boundaries between New Rochelle's neighbors—Pelham, Larchmont, Eastchester, and Scarsdale—this one was created in the 1920s when the New Rochelle Art Association commissioned resident notable artists—like Norman Rockwell, Remington Schuyler, Coles Phillips, and others—to "bound" the town with their creativity. The prolific comic strip artist Clare Briggs naturally chose his most popular cartoon character, the "Feller," 19-teens America's most recognizable "bad"—but-not-so-bad—boy. He brought the Feller to life in both images and words; the dozens of ditties accompanying the drawings in his 1914 *When a Feller Needs a Friend* address all sorts of subjects, but many address the Feller's tendency to be tongue-tied. A youth this fresh and untested can be forgiven his falling far short of Demosthenes or Dante in the art of declaration; but when he brings his experience in line with his convictions, the Feller is surprisingly eloquent, if altogether homely:

A Real Calamity

There ain't no charity anywheres,
There ain't a single soul that cares,
There ain't a person wants a boy
To have th' slightest bit o' joy.
I lost my nickel; I can't go
To see th' movin' picture show,
But all th' world goes right along
As if there wasn't nothin' wrong.

Wet, tired, slightly bored, passed in each Westchester County town by hundreds of luxury SUVs an hour, the highway walker heartily echoes the Feller's complaint: all the world *does* go right along as if there wasn't nothin' wrong. Still, we should be happy, because we are out-of-doors:

Saturday Morning

Spotty Burk, he's gone a-fishin',
Warts Malone's out on his bike—
Huh! There ain't no good a-wishin'
I could do one thing I like.
When I'm growed up, then you'll see me
Livin' always out-o-doors.

Hermit Dan—say, that will be me
With no carpets on my floors.

In Concord in the 1820s, or New Rochelle in the 1920s, and every American town in every decade in between, the Feller faced one boundary that superseded all others:

UNDER THE BAN

Why is it rich folks' little girls
With dandy clo'es an' nifty curls
Can't come a-near us poor folks' boys
Without their nurses makes a noise
An' yells an' calls them back so quick
As if they thought we'd make 'em sick?
Th' funny part is, rich kids fuss
Because they want to play with us.

Henry—and this cartoon Feller too, one suspects—was a village boy, son of, if not a bourgeois town father, at least a fortunate, even favored, citizen. A bedroom village (perhaps the premier bedroom village, just forty-five minutes by train from midtown Manhattan), New Rochelle in the 1920s was full of little girls with nifty curls, and full of nurses and nannies who could be counted on to make a noise when class boundaries were crossed by their young charges. Clare Briggs had it dead right when he said that rich kids oblivious to class prejudices were keen to play with those of more modest means.

In November 1925, New Rochelle became celebrated—or notorious—as a place where certain Fellers would certainly *not* find a friend. National newspapers were filled with sensational headlines about the *Rhinelander v. Rhinelander* trial. Twenty-one-year-old Leonard "Kip" Rhinelander—the scion of the wealthy and socially prominent New York City Rhinelander family, who traced their ancestry back to the original French Huguenot settlers of New Rochelle in 1686—had married Alice Jones, a domestic who was the daughter of working-class English immigrants. After the *New Rochelle Standard Star* ran a story headlined "Rhinelander Marries Daughter of Colored Man" (Alice's chauffeur father was of mixed race), and metropolitan region papers picked it up, Kip Rhinelander's father demanded that his son leave his wife and sign an annulment complaint prepared by the father's attorneys, which asserted that Alice had lured Rhinelander into marriage by hiding her race.

Stumbling on the story of this revealing social scandal *after* I had walked through New Rochelle, I was not at all surprised. Along the Kings Highway and Old Post Road and the tributary streets and avenues of New Rochelle, one sniffs, along with the slight tang of salt air, a pronounced aroma of aristocracy, elitism, and privilege. Even if Mexican bodegas and package stores now outnumber the boutiques and barbershops, one can't miss that this village's boundary work did not end in the seventeenth century when the Huguenots settled here—after the local Lenape Indians were displaced. There are far too many country clubs, beach clubs, and athletic clubs (New Rochelle is home to the "country" location of the New York Athletic Club,

America's premier patrician sportsmen's club) not to alert the wakeful walker to the town's snobby past. By 1925, after two or three generations of African American servants, gardeners, liverymen, and then chauffeurs who needed to be quartered close at hand, some lovesick son of a Gilded Age tycoon was bound to fall for a domestic's daughter. Alice Jones stepped too far too fast—and paid the price.

The tacit rules for just who might speak up just where in 1920s exurbia may have been invisible, but they were maniacally enforced. Alice, however fair her skin color or respected her father might be, was sentenced to silence from birth. When Alice's attorney, the eloquent and able Lee Parson Jones, spoke up for her in order to procure justice, he did so in righteous indignation at the cruel, casual racism of former New York Supreme Court judge Isaac Mills. In the ensuing decades, New Rochelle's "boundary work" would be done via zoning regulations and school segregation. Clare Briggs's Feller was white; Norman Rockwell's RICH IN HISTORY welcome sign showed white Continental soldiers on their way to the Battle of White Plains; THE PASSING OF THE BRITISH UNDER LORD HOWE, OCT. 18, 1776—cartoonist Coles Phillips's sign near New Rochelle's Eastchester border—depicts British troops leaving New York under the command of General Howe. The welcome signs suggest that no nonwhite folks ever darkened New Rochelle's door.

The Feller was also a boy. Well, I'm a boy too, with a white male—Henry Thoreau—as my hero, but he had universal suffrage and equality as ideas and ideals. I've lectured in university classrooms on the darkest moments in American social history, and written texts for wayside historical markers, but it takes fifty years—or never—for truth-telling to leak out from scholar-ship to the streets and public historical consciousness. That Clare Briggs's welcome sign could stand (and even be refur-bished, along with the nine other signs, ten years ago—to the tune of $70,000) at the Pelham–New Rochelle border on the Kings Highway is a testament to how poorly we have adopted Henry's manifesto to "crow like a chanticleer in the morning" about racial, social, and economic injustice, or even at least get a bit more honest about the sins scattered throughout our na-tional past. In America there has long been a thin line separat-ing civic national mythology from vapid boosterism, insipid sentimentalism, and a certain feel-good-at-any-costs imperative.

$$\mathcal{B}$$

HENRY THOREAU'S ESSAY "Walking" is as much about *speaking* as it is about walking, and it is also—in true Thoreauvian fashion—as much about *not speaking* as speaking. "I wish," he begins, "to speak a word for Nature, for absolute freedom and wildness . . ." Ever since this essay was published, just one month before he died at age forty-four, readers have mistaken it for a *naturalist* credo, a call to embrace nature as the ground of all being, of all joy, of all goodness. This is the complete oppo-site of what Thoreau intended. "Walking"—its twenty-two thousand words interrupted one-fourth of the way through by "The Old Marlborough Road," a self-evident poetic underscor-ing of his true allegiance—is as clear a credo of spiritualist (in the sense of a bedrock belief in the reality of the spiritual world) sympathy as any nineteenth century surveyor, pencil tinkerer, and gifted amateur naturalist ever mustered. "I am a mystic, transcendentalist, and natural philosopher to boot," Henry declared in answer to the American Association for the Advancement of Science questionnaire mailed to him in 1854.

From Broadway to Walden, no one could ever quite tell me what a "transcendentalist" was. Indeed, they could not even bring themselves to say it; it was the amorphous entity "transcendentalism" or plural "transcendentalists," but never the single *transcendentalist*. "They believed there was something transcending nature," echoed the tautological refrain. Henry did not like the word "something"; neither do I. It is not a helpful aid to speaking, but a dodge, a half thought, even if it does speak volumes about the nature of that thought. Just like a real naturalist out botanizing in the Concord or Maine woods who names species, not "some plants," the true spiritual pilgrim afoot on the Old Marlborough Road can name the individual organisms he encounters. Henry made it as plain as day what sort of walker he was—a walker *out of bounds*, including the biggest boundary of all, that which we moderns call "nature," as we tightly circumscribe the cosmos into the tiger cage called the "physical world." "Walking," and *Walden*, and all of Henry's speaking, were uttered to *enlarge* that cage, to bust it wide open, in fact, to encompass the Old Marlborough Road's boundless denizens.

A thousand feet from where the Kings Highway joins the Post Road to Boston, set back off the Post Road farther than any Carnegie Library that I have ever seen, is a massive gray granite neoclassical beauty, with a pair of oversized Corinthian columns flanking the entrance, and a grand fanlight above this.

Oddly, where NEW ROCHELLE PUBLIC LIBRARY should be, spanning the pair of pediments, just under a sculpture of a Greek lamp, it reads instead HAGEDORN. There is no book drop-off box out front, there are no patrons pouring in and out, their arms loaded with books.

Andrew Carnegie gave New Rochelle $60,000 in 1910 to build a new library, and this grand edifice was finished in 1914. It was home to Norman Rockwell's first exhibit. When publisher Christopher Hagedorn bought it for $150,000 in 1994, the windows were boarded up with plywood, and graffiti was spray-painted across the façade. The city had built a new library, and left this old gem to crumble like the coal pile in the basement.

In 1994, not a single New Rochelle resident recalled that in the years when it was being built, a pair of "Fellers" used to serve as sidewalk superintendents and gofers for the construction crew. To thank them for their help, when the library opened in 1914, ten-year-old Joe and twelve-year-old Charley Campbell were given library cards that admitted them to the stacks—a privilege otherwise restricted to adult scholars. By the time he was seventeen, Joe had read every one of the mammoth ethnological reports of the Smithsonian Institution's Bureau of American Ethnology. When he wrote in his diary about the secret society he'd started in New Rochelle, he made no mention of his sources for the rites and rituals—Frank Cushing on the Zuni; Truman Michelson on the Fox; John Wesley Powell on the Numa. Joe's journal records his building a telescope to study stars and birds, and how he adored Douglas Fairbanks films. His idea of the hero was a cross between Fairbanks and

Leonardo da Vinci; Joe was lettering in track at the exclusive
Canterbury School in New Milford, Connecticut, and along
with playing mandolin, guitar, piano, and trumpet, he loved to
sculpt and paint. He also loved to write; his journal was his
workshop for that craft to which he perhaps came first and most
naturally. Surely he had kissed the Blarney Stone, for words
flowed effortlessly from him.

Can you imagine Henry Thoreau watching TV? It's a scene
too comic—or tragic—for words. If we cannot imagine Henry in
front of the boob tube, why put ourselves there? I haven't owned
a television for thirty years, but the last TV show I remember
was one I watched with a circle of friends in 1988. Each Sunday
we would get the TV out of the closet and place it on a stand in
an empty room that was serving as a dance studio at the time,
and watch Bill Moyers and eighty-three-year-old Joseph Campbell converse about world mythology. After each hour-long encounter, we all—each of us from different faith traditions (my
wife had been a nun for sixteen years)—felt lifted up, ennobled,
expanded, Moyers's Baptist-minister gravity making just the
right ballast for Campbell's glib Irish Catholic levity. Bringing
these TV conversations—which were faithfully watched by
thirty million viewers—to mind now, I wonder what music the
producers used to supplement the two voices, to swell any surge
of emotion the two men set in motion.

Going to YouTube to answer my question, I click on the
opening episode, "The Hero's Adventure," and as the trumpets
and tympani sound, and five masks—African, Greek, Pacific
Northwest Coast Native American, Chinese, and some uniden-

tifiable other—converge on a background of stardust, the title
appears in golden letters:

JOSEPH CAMPBELL
                              AND
                                        THE POWER OF MYTH

I misremembered or mistook what we'd been watching back in
1988. The epic PBS broadcast was not a documentary series
about world mythology so much as a heavily edited, effusively
scored, Bill Moyers–facilitated mythologization of Joseph Campbell, late twentieth century cosmonaut of the "Inner Reaches of
Outer Space"—the title of the 1981 four-lecture symposium delivered by Campbell in the great hall of San Francisco's Palace of
Fine Arts, where Campbell shared the platform with astronaut
Rusty Schweickart. *The Power of Myth* was a MacArthur
Foundation-and-PBS-sponsored thinking man's space opera,
the inevitable public television sequel to George Lucas's 1977
Star Wars, which drew its own "Force" from Campbell's 1949
opus *The Hero with a Thousand Faces*. The series had largely
been filmed at Lucas's Skywalker Ranch in California.

After the music and masks of that opening curtain, the be-
spectacled Moyers appears in a drab gray suit and brown tie, to
tell a story about Joe Campbell's favorite story, of Campbell's
having overheard a Shinto priest telling an American delegate
to a world religion conference: "We don't have an ideology. We
dance."

Joe Campbell was married for forty-nine years to the dancer
and choreographer Jean Erdman. He loved to watch dance,
loved to talk about dance, to profess about dance. But Joe

Campbell did not himself dance. We who watched those six hours of the PBS series would do well to keep that in mind when we encounter Campbell's books or any of the many other cultural productions—from *Star Wars* to the latest space western fantasy—that have Campbell's ideology as their foundation. For, despite Bill Moyers's opening assertion that "Joseph Campbell was one of the most spiritual men I ever met," the Feller from New Rochelle was a silver-tongued ideologist, a peddler of the most easily accepted of modern lies—that mythology is just a story, that the gods are human inventions, rather than the reverse.

"But he didn't have an ideology, or a theology," Moyers continued in his characterization of Campbell. "Mythology was to him the song of the universe, the music of the spheres, so deeply embedded in our collective unconscious that we *dance* to it, even when we can't name the tune." Here Moyers comes close to the truth, if the mythology to which he was referring was the one peddled by PBS in this most-watched-ever TV series. Joseph Campbell may have died just a few months before the PBS series aired, but we are still dancing to *his* tune, and it is a deadly, soul-destroying one.

"I walk out," Henry wrote in "Walking," "into a nature such as the old prophets and poets, Menu, Moses, Homer, Chaucer walked in. You may name it America, but it is not America. There is a truer account of it in mythology, than in a history of America, so called, than I have seen." Then comes "The Old Marlborough Road." There *is* a road from Marlborough to Concord called just that; I have walked that one and could point it out to you on a map. But this Old Marlborough Road is no cousin to the Kings Highway or the Boston Post Road. It is all *celestial, supersensible,* a narrow and still yet narrowing path found on no map or gazetteer. "Nobody repairs it, / For nobody wears it," Henry tells us, and then:

> It is a living way,
> As the Christians say.

Joe Campbell loved to speak about the "dynamic of life," and he certainly was well tutored in a certain strain of biology— ostensibly the study of life and the living. At Dartmouth College and then at Columbia University, he studied with such leaders of American biology as William Patten and E. B. Wilson, and abandoned his family's Roman Catholicism for Darwinism. Campbell took up the materialist study of life just at the moment when all philosophical misgivings about a strictly physical explanation of the Creation were cast aside. Six months after the Rhinelander trial America would be swept up in the sensation of the Scopes "Monkey" trial, which, at least for liberal America, put the final nail in the coffin of the Christian conception of biology.

Though, after transferring from Dartmouth to Columbia, Joe Campbell switched his major from biology to literature, he continued to have a deep interest in, and particular conception of, the study of life. In one section of *The Power of Myth*, Campbell—reaching out with both of his big hands down to his solar plexus, then bringing them up in front of his heart— declares: "The *daimonic* is a Greek word and it refers to the dynamic of life. Your *daimon* is the dynamic of your life. And we are *so against* the dynamic of life in our tradition that we turned it into a *devil!*" In those ten seconds of tape, Joseph Campbell totally corrupts both the ancient Greek concept of the *daimon*, and twenty centuries of Western cultural history. In ancient Greece, *daimon* referred to actual spiritual beings, particularly those beings who wed themselves closely to individuals, imparting to the individual human life its unmistakable and unique character. By Thoreau's time, the word had become— like "genius," the Roman tutelary spirit—mere metaphor for one's character and disposition.

Henry's biology, perhaps more strictly termed "natural history," though practiced a century before Campbell's, encompassed a much wider sphere of life. The attentive reader of Thoreau will find accounts and hints everywhere of his observations of the wildest creatures of field and forest:

> *Not many there be,*
> *Who enter therein,*
> *Only the guests of the*
> *Irishman Quin.*

Joe Campbell's father's father had come over from Ireland at the end of the potato famine, and became a gardener on a Waltham, Massachusetts, estate. Even though he said that "the whole fairyland world of Europe is out of Ireland" (which surely it is not), he knew not those "respectable folks" of the Old Marlborough Road familiar and friendly with Henry's neighbor Quin. Henry looked far into the future when he wrote, about the Old

Marlborough Road: "Possibly the day will come when it will be partitioned off into so-called pleasure grounds, in which a few will take a narrow and exclusive pleasure only . . . and walking over the surface of God's earth shall be construed to mean trespassing on some gentleman's grounds."

Walk through New Rochelle—or Concord, or any prosperous American town from the Atlantic to the Pacific—today, and you instantly see that we have gone merrily about manifesting exactly that nightmarish landscape of gated pleasure grounds against which Henry warned 150 years ago. That the Elysian fields he happily trod, and to which he sought ever to wake his neighbors up, should be not merely gated, but forsaken, was, I believe, beyond even his imagination of the evil days ahead. Joseph Campbell's popularity, the persistence of the monocultural Campbellian outlook on the treasure house of Elysium that is world mythology, calls for someone to speak up and out. Having walked a mile or two in Joseph Campbell's moccasins, I hope that I might do so. We both played mandolin, ran cross-country, and fell in love with American Indians in grade school. We both studied biology at Dartmouth (having both been drawn there because of the school's roots in Eleazar Wheelock's Indian "academy"). We even (almost; we're one day apart) share the same birthday. Surely I too have kissed the Blarney Stone. As a historian I know better than to find too much fault in Campbell's well-documented racism, sexism, anti-Semitism, and Reagan-era country club conservatism. I might even forgive him his sloppy scholarship, his tendency toward circular reasoning, and his superficial and mostly selfish speaking style.

What cannot be forgiven, given its profound continuing effect on the souls of young people, is Joseph Campbell's rendering of the "hero's journey." With ample help from Bill Moyers and George Lucas and his many Hollywood imitators (a seven-page "Hero's Journey Outline" memo written by a Disney screenwriter in the mid-eighties became the formulaic template taught in dozens of American film schools), Campbell's flat and spectacularly false conception of human biography and its dance with the spiritual world has become a cosmopolitan industry that turns the greatest story ever told into trope and mere metaphor while churning out blockbuster film fantasies. Would that Bill Moyers had devoted one episode of *The Power of Myth* to going out and interviewing any one of the peoples whose myths Campbell so blithely threw into his big iron monomyth melting pot. Each and every tribe and tradition past and present would have taken the greatest offense, to be told that their revered portraits of the world beyond the physical were just so many pretty pictures, whose details could be substituted from one place and time to another.

Joseph Campbell spoke about one hero vastly more often than all of the others in world mythology. Whether the theme was birth, death, "the call," sacrifice, bliss, or eternity, Jesus Christ got more airplay on Campbell's All the Heroic Hits, All the Time World Myth station than Odysseus, Osiris, Icarus, Buddha, Parsifal, or even Han Solo and Luke Skywalker. Despite holding forth on public television, Campbell's caricatured Christ was very much an AM radio version, starting with His patently borrowed—from previous myths—birth:

which has not a single sentence out of painstakingly chosen place—in service to his higher purpose. On a "reduced plan" showing the depths of Walden Pond and two topographic profiles, in characteristically careful fashion, Thoreau noted the location of the Fitchburg Railroad, his cabin, and two nearby hills, and listed the area, circumference, and greatest width, length, and depth of the pond. Though he never draws attention to it in the text, the two cross-sectional lines describe a perfect cross, nearly the dimensions of the Christian crucifix. Thoreau's *gita—Walden*—immortalized Walden Pond as an emblem for truth, and his survey echoed this in its mapping of a universal law of nature. Strict draftsman that he was, he could in full faith inscribe these two axes upon the outline of the pond.

Thoreau's repugnance for the Church never affected his devotion to Christ. In *A Week on the Concord and Merrimack Rivers* he said, "Christ was a sublime actor on the stage of the world. He knew what he was thinking when he said, 'Heaven and earth shall pass away, but my words shall not pass away.' I draw close to him at such a time." Thoreau identified with Christ, the fellow heretic and fool, not only as a historical figure but as a living presence whom he had experienced intensely in the dark of winter in his Walden cabin. "It is necessary not to be a Christian, to appreciate the beauty and significance of the life of Christ," Thoreau declared.

When Joseph Campbell spoke of Jesus Christ's virgin birth, the healing miracles, or the sacrifice on Golgotha, he gave no historical or metahistorical context, nor much in the way of illuminating detail. Truly, most of the time it was just straight blarney, spiced up by allusions to *Finnegans Wake* or *Star Wars*, or some personal anecdote. One moment Campbell is quoting Jesus's "I and the Father are one," and the next he is telling a story about being out to dinner in New Rochelle's neighboring Bronxville one Thursday night ("maids' night off in Bronxville, so that many of the families were out in restaurants") and overhearing a father and son arguing over the boy's refusal to drink his tomato juice. The mother intervenes, and finally the father explodes: "He can't go through life doing what he wants to do. If he does only what he wants to do, he'll be dead. Look at me. I've never done a thing I wanted to in all my life."

Campbell tells Moyers that he thought: "My God, there's Babbitt incarnate," and that he recognized that the man had never "followed his bliss." Then he piles the blarney on, as he sketches a glib "grab it" philosophy and theology of bliss. "Poets are simply those who have made a profession and lifestyle of being in touch with their bliss." "Are you going to think of fortune, or are you going to think of your bliss?" "The religious people tell us we really won't experience bliss until we die and go to heaven. But I believe in having as much bliss as you can of the experience while you are still alive."

Knowing how incredibly cruel and judgmental Joseph Campbell could be to his Sarah Lawrence students who protested the Vietnam War—he automatically failed activist students—and how harshly he ranted about the hedonism of his sixties-era students, it is unnerving to hear Campbell speak out such a "liberal" credo. When the mild-mannered, obviously pietistic former Baptist minister Moyers asks Campbell what he thinks of the man who seems to have stumbled in following his bliss, and who might be muddling through without it, Campbell replies: "Yes, he is the one that evokes compassion, the poor chap. To see him stumbling around when all the waters of life are right there really evokes one's pity."

Ernest and intent as ever, Moyers musters his most fervent plea for this living, breathing Obi-Wan Kenobi: "The waters of life are right there? Where?" For seasoned viewers of public television, it is a deeply familiar moment, Moyers the middle-aged Luke Skywalker, in danger of himself becoming Babbitt, beseeching Obi-Wan for the magic key to self-transformation. "Wherever you are," Campbell assures him, "if you are following your bliss, you are enjoying that refreshment, that life within you, all the time."

Use the force, Luke! Let go!

ℬ

SOME FUTURE CULTURAL HISTORIAN may look back upon both Lucas's *Star Wars* and PBS's *The Power of Myth* as twin bellwethers of a sort, signaling the late twentieth century extinction of the Western *My*steries, and simultaneously the birth of a ravenous popular appetite for *my*steries. In the absence of a living relationship to the beings of the spiritual world—saints, angels, archangels, powers, dominions, and the diminutive "respectable folks" of nature—America, and then with it the entire modern world, has substituted a simulacrum of endless intergalactic battle scenes as backdrop for cartoon heroes to employ a blind, Nietzschean "Force" to triumph over heavily armed external enemies. When the preeminent interpreter of the world corpus of deeds of spiritual beings manifests in a Joseph Campbell or a

George Lucas, one can be certain that God is not dead, but that the human intellect is exhausted and dead, and that something, some quality, even some new creature and creation, is about to be born.

In Henry's day, those seeking to birth the new (hu)man being were abandoning the exhausted mysteries of clubby Freemasonry for charismatic cults from Mormonism to "Millerism" (followers of William Miller, who later founded the Seventh-day Adventist Church). Almost every one of these had a male "prophet" at its center who claimed to receive divine revelation. As a young "Feller" living across the street from Concord's principal Freemason Lodge, Henry had peeked in on those mock mysteries and found them wanting; instead of trying to bind the gods to appear through oaths and empty theater, he built his own temple out in the Walden woods, confident that the gods would visit him there. He was not disappointed. They are still out there, waiting for us.

In order to meet and befriend the infinite gossamer beings of the Old Marlborough Road, one must truly leave the Kings Highway and Old Post Road and *all* the "Broadways" for the narrow crepuscular path of self-examination, even self-mortification. Blissful soul that he was, Henry's asceticism was a happy one, and for every bodily pleasure he may have denied himself, there were ten he fully enjoyed. Huckleberries, sunbathing, walking in wonder—these erotic delights were front and center in his yoga. Through them Henry experienced "I and the Father are one" in a manner unknown to Joseph Campbell.

Few if any of Joseph Campbell's admirers realize that he is responsible for introducing America to a particular understanding of the Eastern chakra system. In 1942, Campbell attended German indologist Heinrich Zimmer's Columbia University lectures on Indian metaphysics; after the Nazis stripped him of his University of Heidelberg post in 1938, Zimmer had moved to New Rochelle, and he and Campbell became close friends. When Zimmer died in 1943, Campbell edited and published his writings on Hindu tantra. But even before his encounter with Zimmer, Campbell had taken a deep interest in kundalini yoga via his encounter with Swami Nikhilananda (1895–1973), who had founded the Ramakrishna-Vivekananda Center in New York City in 1933.

If one examines Campbell's publications beyond *The Power of Myth* one discovers the real roots of his "follow your bliss" credo—in kundalini yoga. Throughout his scholarship and popular writing runs the deep vein of the lotus flowers and their activity. Unfortunately, just as with his study of world mythology, Campbell's presentation of the human organs for spiritual perception is badly, tragically misconceived. In publications from the 1958 *Myths to Live By* to the posthumous *The Inner Reaches of Outer Space: Metaphor as Myth and as Religion* (1988), Campbell put forward a simplistic, if not totally erroneous, interpretation of the chakras. The root chakra he associated with "spiritual torpor," and "holding on to a life that is no life at all because there is no joy in it, no vitality in it, but just grim, dogged existence." The root chakra, Campbell clearly believed, was the root of Babbittry! The third chakra, the solar plexus, Campbell associated with "conquest and defeat, whether military, financial, or erotic"—the seat of the "will to power." In the heart chakra, the fourth, resided all "powers of art and the spirit." At the fifth—throat—chakra, "all interpositions between oneself and the vision of God" could be purified and removed.

To fully narrate the history of the intersection of Joseph Campbell and the American "New Age," one would leave New Rochelle and the Old Post Road for the central California coast, Route 1, the Esalen Institute, and the shimmering savanna of wild live oaks—from Jean Houston and Joan Halifax to Sam Keen and Stanley Keleman, Michael Murphy and Stan and Christina Grof—from whom Campbell drew inspiration, and in turn inspired. Joe Campbell was a troubadour, a serial inspirer, to be sure. The problem with troubadours, if they are not fully rooted in an authentic Mystery tradition, is that they inspire erroneous impulses and ideas. The explosion in America of promiscuous, pop-psychological, patently false expositions of the chakras, which were reduced to meaningless tokens by a long line of New Age authors and teachers, can rightfully be laid at the charismatic troubadour Joe Campbell's feet, and Esalen's seductive redwood and madrone threshold.

The vivacious and inquisitive "Feller" Joe Campbell had uncanny tracking instincts, like those Indian hunters he loved so dearly. He tracked his way to an American family with fairyland Irish ancestry and tradition, and to a town blessed by prosperity, gentility, and refined intellectuality. He even managed to place himself alongside an august temple of learning—complete with sculpted Aladdin's lamp above the door—just as it was being built. All the ensuing intellectual and cultural loci of his life express the hallmark of an initiate, of being in the right place at the right time. Certainly, when he left the backwaters of

Dartmouth for Columbia, where he became the student of Roger Sherman Loomis, one of the world's most respected authorities on Arthurian literature, Campbell was one cunning hunter. Before his explorations and expositions of *all* the traditions, he chose a very particular one, the Grail tradition. His 1927 Columbia University master's thesis, titled "A Study of the Dolorous Stroke," boldly took on the most prominent scholars of the previous half century, promising to go where no knight of knowledge had gone before. "Modern questers for the secrets of the Grail," wrote the twenty-three-year-old Joe Campbell in the opening to his thesis, "swarm along a well-worn route, and battle their way through the multitude around them." Not so the impeccable quester Campbell! He would know the pristine, ur-significance of the Grail tale's "dolorous stroke," by virtue of his own heroic quest through the wilds of world mythology, where the intellect would be buffeted and harassed by a thousand parallels and precedents. Joe would mount his trusty horse Passat and go boldly into the fray, surviving jousting javelin and swinging sword to pierce through to Universal Truth, in the doing running roughshod over Sir James Frazer, Jessie ("Miss J. L.") Weston, Alfred Nutt, Arthur E. Waite, and his own adviser, Professor Roger Loomis.

Character by character, not just in his 1927 thesis but throughout his long career, Joe Campbell also ran roughshod over every aspect of the Grail romance. Campbell either ascribes erroneous historical precedents to the Grail personages, or else dismisses them wholesale as fictions. For Campbell, it is all about "materials" and "analogies," *not* spiritual realities. Because Gahmuret flies a flag with an anchor on a green field, he must really be an exiled prince, Sultan Shah of Aleppo, because this fellow sported the same standard. Anfortas is not *like* the wounded Christ, but *is* the wounded Christ, thanks to Campbell's collapsing of categories. Kundrie is just a Western remaking of the Hindu goddess Kali. The piebald Feirefiz is an exact copy of the Muslim warrior-prince Qutb-ud-din Aibak. The Grail knights "can only" have gotten their vow of absolute anonymity from the Muhammadan assassins. Buddha's famed stone begging bowl, amalgamated with a greenstone relic of San Lorenzo, becomes the Holy Grail. "Arthur" is a river that has Lake Geneva as its source. Blarney!

Unmitigated, promiscuous, mendacious blarney, all of it! And to think that thirty million kids have watched—and believed!—Peter Joseph's *Zeitgeist* films, which have their intellectual and spiritual roots in such poppycock as this!

The Virgin birth is a *symbol* to Joseph Campbell; the Crucifixion is a *symbol*; the Last Supper, Night in Gethsemane, Ascension, Pentecost, all the healing miracles are mere *symbols*. This is Joseph Campbell's great and unforgivable heresy. Christianity— and every step of Christ's life—is *a mystical fact*, with cosmic consequences for all eternity. There is nothing in the least "symbolic" about a single one of those steps! As a key to the meaning of the elusive and enigmatic Grail quest, Campbell offers the Buddhist "legend" of Gautama. How in the world can an avatar who is wholly new, superseding all the world's past avatars, be "explained" by a historically prior avatar, like Buddha?

All the loci of Joseph Cambell's life—especially his studies— express the hallmark of an initiate. But despite being immersed in the Grail, and studying very particularly the Grail story, he missed Christ, and initiation. This is incredibly telling for our time, for us, who cannot count on a whispered invitation to initiation *by an initiate*. It is indeed a *dolorous stroke* that the sum of Joseph Campbell's scholarship and teaching claims that the dolorous stroke is merely the Christian narrative metamorphosis of an ancient Oriental tale. At twenty-three, Joe's pronouncements were as confident and cockeyed as they'd be when served up by Bill Moyers's saintly TV sage: "The dolorous stroke . . . has run its course, and totters now at the edge of its grave." Here was the great appeal of Campbell's monomyth monomania; as universal as he wanted a myth to be, when it served *his* storytelling purpose, he would in an instant declare its death, since it was all *just story*.

If consummate quester Joe Campbell could miss that the Holy Grail was Christ—the Son of God—he could certainly miss recognizing that the lotus flowers, those sublime and mysterious organs of the human astral body, are a Christ-given birthright to every human being, whose essence consists of primal thoughts from the Father God. The seven seals of the Apocalypse are the seven lotus flowers. The transfiguration of Jesus Christ on Mount Tabor was the opening and penetration of Jesus of Nazareth's lotus flowers by the power of Christ radiating through them. Temptation is the improper development of the lotus flowers. Saints are human beings whose lotus flowers have been transfigured by the Christ power pouring through them. The I AM—the esoteric name of Christ-power that transfigures the lotus flowers—is the source of the seven healing miracles described in the Gospels. The crown chakra—the lotus flower above the head—creates one's connection with the spiritual world, appearing to those who can perceive it as a fireworks of a thousand scintillating violet sparks. Bearing the human's eternal name, this lotus flower contains within itself all the consequences of one's positive karma. Eight-petaled, the upper part of this lotus flower connects the human being with his angel, while the lower part streams down past the two-petaled third eye chakra to the feet as a purifying, ennobling stream. The "washing of the feet" is no universal mythic "trope," but a universal Christ-imparted supersensible physiological *reality* whose effects can easily be seen in such walking saints as Christ, Francis, Sister Elizabeth Ann Seton (this first American-born saint was from New Rochelle!), and Henry Thoreau. Their feet, which carry them and us toward the future, are literally *holy*.

There is much of the Mars chakra, the sixteen-petaled throat lotus flower, that is expressed in the biography and character of Henry Thoreau, and of those who have—like Mahatma Gandhi and Martin Luther King Jr.—followed his example. The throat chakra is unsurprisingly the lotus flower of the word, and the Word. Hovering in the subtle body in the region of the larynx, it has petals that rotate once per hour. While Emerson and other admired antebellum orators often lectured for two hours or more, the Mars-blessed Henry instinctively kept his addresses to under an hour—the period of the throat chakra's rotation.

This lotus flower holds the promise not just of magical speech, but of magical listening, attuning itself perfectly to the words of the Father, Son, Holy Spirit, and the Persona—not a Campbellian "mask," but the true higher angelic self of each and every human being. Rightly disciplined, it cognizes the genesis and birth of the Four Hierarchies, and the Four

Elements, through which it can give and receive magical forces. Speaking on and for the Earth and for Christ, it becomes part of the World Word.

Here, as we leave New Rochelle and its Fellers for farther points along the Old Post Road and the Old Marlborough Road both, I would find a quiet hillside to show you a suite of seven gestures and movements that can put all seven of Christ's healing miracles and His accompanying Words—from "I AM the true vine" at the root chakra to "I AM the Resurrection and the Life" at the crown—deep inside you. But about this road-borne lesson considering Fellers speaking, it is time to speak no more. A Feller knows that there is all the time in the world to get to where we are going, and many friends along the way. For now, as we pass into Larchmont under Remington Schuyler's FOUNDED BY THE HUGUENOTS—1688 sign showing a group of Indian hunters striding along this very Boston Post Road, we remember that angels do not shout but whisper, and that all right speech and right action are preceded by deep and attentive right listening.

"Read not the Times," said Henry. "Read the Eternities." Stand apart from the mob. Be wary of anything—books, films, ideas—that is merely "popular." Avoid glibness, and give the glib tavern speaker and tavern keeper both a wide berth for their inanities. A Feller must be mighty wary not to wake up one day and find himself one more Babbitt or Dilbert.

Put up your own signs and markers. Make them mirthful, inviting, and easily read, but by all means, make them *true*. Seek out those places and people from whom you can cultivate a sure sense of the *eternal*, so that you might effortlessly bar the commonplace *times* from your speech and listening, ever-wakeful ear.

Only through listening on the one hand, and through hearing and proclaiming on the other, does something new arise in the spiritual world and on the Earth. *Walden*'s every word is inscribed there. So can our words be, if only we strive to know more than we say.

#2: SPEAK, always striving to know more than you say.

CHAPTER 3

Learn to DANCE!

Mrs. Ricketson, playing at her piano, struck into "The Campbells Are Coming." Thoreau put down his book and began to dance—a sylvan dance, as of a faun among rocks and bushes in a sort of labyrinthine fashion, now leaping over obstacles, then advancing with stately strides, returning in curves, then coming back in leaps.   —EDWARD WALDO EMERSON (1917)

E DWARD EMERSON HAD GROWN UP watching his dear friend Henry "dance." When Edward's father was off in New York or London lecturing, Henry would come and see not just to the pressing tasks of garden and woodlot, but to the Emerson children's fancies. Edward and his sister Ellen did their own ritual dance whenever they heard the side door open as Henry stepped in with a load of cordwood in his arms, to tumble into the wood box at the bottom of the stairs. At that sound, they would appear on the top landing and beckon Henry up to play with them. Nearly fifty years after Henry's death, when Edward recollected the image of the capering Henry in the Ricketsons' New Bedford parlor, he pointed out that the mischievous dancer deliberately stepped on Bronson Alcott's toes to get his all-too-serious goat.

In the last year of his life, sent westward by a physician as a cure for his festering case of consumption, having traveled up the Minnesota River to the Redwood Sioux Agency, Henry had a chance to see a performance of the Dream Dance, an elaborate ritual circle dance that had been inspired a decade before by a young girl's visionary experience, when her band had been attacked by a detachment of U.S. cavalry. Perhaps because he was near dying, Thoreau expressed but little interest in the costumed dancers—thirty of them—accompanied by a dozen drummers and others who blew flutes or rhythmically struck their arrows against their bows, keeping "good time," Henry noted.

Both his ability to cut capers in Yankee parlors and his perambulations about Concord and farther afield in the Maine woods or the dunes of Cape Cod showed that Henry knew all about "keeping good time." The vast mysterious but rhythmic dance of life was Thoreau's main trade, his deepest question and most perennial avenue of discovery and revelation. Acutely sensitive to the man-made rhythms—the locomotive upon the steel rails; church bells and factory whistles; music boxes and grandfather clocks; and especially the playing of the wind on the aeolian harp of the telegraph lines—of Concord village, Henry was infinitely more attuned to the silent pulse of nature. His great unfinished "Kalendar" opus, his collation of his brief lifetime of local phenological and life history observation, might be seen as a near-Wagnerian musical score, expressing as best he knew the confluence of the variegated sweet melodies and inexhaustible rhythms of life.

One sensed that inwardly, Henry was always dancing, and that, just as he could not contain himself at the sound of that Scottish jig in the Ricketsons' parlor, his not-infrequent ecstasies were a sort of subtle body ballet, a cosmic dance. Threading his way through a spruce swamp on one "aggravated November day" in December 1855, when a flock of lesser redpolls flew by, he suddenly felt:

> My body is all sentient. As I go here or there, I am tickled by this or that I come in contact with, as if I touched the wires of a battery. I can generally recall—have fresh in my mind—several scratches last received. These I continually recall to mind, reimpress, and harp upon. The age of miracles is thus returned . . .
>
> I am surprised and enchanted often by some quality which I cannot detect. I have seen an attribute of another world and condition of things.

If you have ever walked alone a long distance—five or ten miles in a day will do; it need not be twenty miles and more—you have had that rush of gooseflesh spread from your torso both up to your scalp and down to your toes, where your whole body too has gone "all sentient." Like Henry's redpoll, when that wave of pleasure comes, it is always some small, quiet, quotidian gesture or scene that triggers it. Examine your inner logbook of such walk-induced ecstasies, and you will no doubt discover a common denominator: before you felt yourself "moved," something—a squirrel, a leaf, a scrap of paper, a gust of wind, a thought—had also *moved*, and set a cascade of simultaneous surrender and self-recollection in motion, as a sympathetic echo. Thanks to my stop in Stamford, I believe I have discovered the subtle physiology, chemistry, and physics of gooseflesh. The *OED* definition only helps to highlight how poorly understood this homely but accurate metaphor is.

> *goose flesh n.* a pimply state of the skin with the hairs erect, produced by cold or fright.

What? This *OED* entry does *not* give me gooseflesh, though it is frightfully cold and dead as a doornail—another elegant compound construction. *My* gooseflesh, your gooseflesh, is hardly "pimply," and though our hairs (papillae) are indeed erect, they rise to attention not from fright or freezing, but from the frisson of something sublime.

GOOSEFLESH

Do geese get goose flesh
When thoughts sublime
Arise to take them out of Time?
Can it be said where
This, titanic wave,
Arises, just what gave
This simple surge, its
Onward push, when geese
Or gods, our flesh do brush?

I wrote this poem after feeling the arctic cold of the frightful beast that is Stamford's downtown, a place so inhuman that it could have manifested only as a symptom of late twentieth century corporate capitalism run amok. To subvert Stamford's gauntlet of concrete bunker parking garages and pedestrian cul-de-sacs I entered town by way of the railroad tracks. Passing the present minimalist/ultra-brutalist rail station, I arrived at a wide switching yard hemmed in by three layers of storm fencing topped by razor wire, rotting storefronts, Caterpillar tractors, and row upon stacked row of concrete culvert pipe about to be laid. I stepped alternately on the creosote crossties and the crushed basalt railroad bed metal, feeling a knot grow in my belly and brain, until I felt short of breath. The Amtrak Acela Express to Boston rushed by just yards away, as I came to a rusted cast-iron switch riveted to a pair of sleepers. Its massive steel spring was spray-painted yellow at one end, and the stout toggle handle, two feet long, hovered at about two o'clock. On both ends, like a rusted industrial yin-yang, the foundry marks, partly broken away, stood out in stamped relief, high enough that they threw shadows in the late afternoon sun:

—AX CORP.
—URN, NY
—2229
—RAGOR

The wave of gooseflesh came from noticing, just six inches away, growing luxuriantly up out of the basalt desert, a big rosette of moth mullein leaves. The tiny white hairs covering each

leaf made the weed light up like a halo, and I felt as if its hairs
were my hair, which at that instant stood up straight on end
from head to toe.

Henry's flesh was the medium by which he made—before
writing it down in his journal—a record of his love, as he practiced the art of reading and responding to the infinite gestures
of the world. Art enlarges understanding by seeking wholes and
then rendering them in figures that will make our flesh dance in
sympathetic response. Henry practiced a physiognomic natural
history in his indefatigable attempt to place himself inside what
he saw, heard, and felt. Trying to imitate the honking of geese,
he instinctively flapped his arms and twisted his head as he uttered "*mow-ack*" in his best nasal twang. His large inventory of
birdcalls had been won by constantly mimicking the little song-
sters. Whenever possible, he felt the fox's foxness, the turtle's
turtleness, the frog's frogness, by leaping or crawling or croak-
ing just like them. His physiognomic science allowed him to see
and speak across structural and functional lines; he thought
that the songs of frogs in late March were not only contemporary with but analogous to the blossoms of the skunk cabbage
and the leafing out of the silver maple.

Henry's physiognomically sensitive flesh took in the railroad
and telegraph and other antebellum technologies and redeemed
them; but he would have been vanquished I think by the Stamford "skyline" of corporate headquarters. The glass and steel
towers stand just far enough apart from one another that there
can be wedged between them a six- or seven-story multilevel
concrete parking garage, so that the workers who enter them
each morning need never step onto a street. This sequestering

is accentuated by the massive, luxurious free dining rooms in each corporate headquarters building, freeing anyone from seeking out lunch fare downtown. Though downtown Stamford is dominated by the million-square-foot Town Center shopping mall, all of the office towers are essentially malls, with inward-looking atriums that they share with the downtown hotels. Standing next to that mullein rosette and the rusted switch on the site of the old New York, New Haven and Hartford Railroad station, looking north across the tracks, you look directly at the slotted wall of the city parking garage, which obscures any view of downtown besides the glorified glass billboards sporting the logos of Aladdin Capital Management ($21.5 billion in assets in 2007); Berkshire Hathaway's Gen Re ($10.5 billion); NBC Sports ($21 billion); UBS, inside which is a trading floor that sustains $1 trillion worth of financial transactions a day (that dubious distinction put the building into the *Guinness World Records*); and GE Capital—too big to quantify.

Though *Scenes from a Mall*, the 1991 Paul Mazursky film starring Bette Midler and Woody Allen, will adequately carica-ture the soul-deadening Stamford Town Center (where most of the shots were filmed), no film captures the "urban renewal" tragedy that in the last twenty-five years erased the entire core of the nineteenth century industrial city that organically and even artfully grew up with the seventeenth century village plan of Stamford. Most of America's first suburbs—Greenwich, Con-necticut; Englewood, New Jersey; Chestnut Hill, Massachu-setts; New Rochelle, New York—were not all white, but made room for servants and workers who were people of color. These early suburbs replicated class spatial patterns of core cities such that the poorest dwelled closest to tiny business districts, while their more affluent white neighbors built commodious homes on spacious grounds at the periphery.

Stamford's poorer section had been right here, adjacent to the old railroad station. But gradually the old spatial hierarchy no longer seemed good enough. A black family in Stamford could move to more elite neighborhoods as they rose through the economic ranks; affluent whites, meanwhile, declared their upward mobility by continuing to move outward centrifugally to all-white suburbs. Like so many other satellite exurban American places, Stamford inexorably turned into a "sundown" town, a village where nonwhite workers were not welcome after the end of the workday. Just down the coast a couple of miles, Darien's exclusive drapery of deluxe homes and yards and automobiles spectacularly displays the demographic and sociological effects of the sundown nightmare.

Step into any of these burghs' cemeteries, and you will see it echoed there. These are "whites-only" burial grounds whose discriminatory tenure stretches from before the Revolution through emancipation to the Voting Rights Act and beyond.

Though, from just about the time of Thoreau's death during the Civil War to the present, Concord has been mythologized as a communitarian village that stood outside Jacksonian-era competitive capitalism (competition that caused his own father's store to fail, sending the family in search of other economic opportunities), it fully participated in the social strains and tensions brought about by expanding American economic life. Stepping away from that striving racket to strive in a more celestial direction when he moved out to Walden Pond, Thoreau had the perfect perspective from which to capture a glimpse of the transition from the harmonious, relatively homogenous Concord in the so-called "Era of Good Feelings" (the post–War of 1812 decades) to the era when the Mill Dam Company—a real estate development concern—contributed to the acceleration of individualistic pursuits among the good people of Concord.

The ghostly traces of the old "liminal" zone of Concord's periphery are caught by Henry in the "Former Inhabitants" section of *Walden*. From Cato Ingraham east of his bean field to Zilpha, whose house had been set ablaze by English soldiers in a War of 1812 raid, to Brister Freeman, whose apple trees planted for his slave master, Thoreau still visited to glean cider apples, these former liminal Concordians are united with Henry in having sought refuge at Concord's margins, though Henry's refugee status was entirely self-selected, while these colored "former inhabitants" had no such luxury of choice. Nutting and Le Grosse and Wyman the Potter and Hugh Quoil are the representative white "outcasts" who shared this quarter of Concord's ample plantation. Whether they were squatters or tax delinquents or ostracized by some more mysterious life circumstance, their remove from the Mill Dam shares fully with Henry's as status symbol of their relative reversal of fortunes in the eyes of the Concord elect.

The Irishman Hugh Quoil, rumored to have been a soldier at Waterloo, came to Walden Woods after an apparent series of misfortunes, for so unlucky was he that his friends pulled down his simple shack after his death, which came within the year after Henry arrived in these same woods. Henry speaks tenderly and fondly of Hugh Quoil, in a way that few of the Mill

Dam folk could ever bring themselves to speak of the "hermit" of Walden Pond.

ℬ

WHEN I WALKED into Stamford, I was possessed of but one odd bit of historical arcana, gathered twenty years before, thanks to my infatuation with the eight elephant folio volumes of the *Linguistic Atlas of New England*, a 1930s research project that aimed, via the field study of vocabulary and pronunciation in two hundred New England towns, to trace back across the Atlantic the interplay of original speech patterns in colonial New England. One of the pair of *LANE* informants in Stamford had been an old Yankee eccentric who had been the brunt of neighborhood boys' cruel practical jokes for over three-quarters of a century, and who rarely left the house. Having found the fieldworker's notes in an archive, I'd learned the bittersweet backstory of a man who was really a good-hearted philanthropist, mistaken as loony and mean by the cruel neighbor boys and their parents alike. This elderly gentleman's fate, as recorded in this unlikely chronicle of small-town interpersonal politics, had stayed with me for two decades, as a window into which I dared not peer further, for I feared what I might find there. A downright promiscuous lover of all boundary crossers, I was myself skittish when the boundary wars were at a misunderstood neighbor's expense, rather than in service of some higher, nobler social goals.

Refreshing my memory and digging a little further into this story of Stamford in the 1930s, I stumbled on the story of

another misfit, someone who had violated community boundaries elsewhere—in New Haven—but here in Stamford had
found wholeness and healing. Having grown up in New Haven,
and having graduated from Yale's Sheffield Scientific School in
1896, Clifford Whittingham Beers was thoroughly familiar
with the Yale "Triennial"—a custom in which Yale University
grads returned to campus three years after graduation to celebrate the class reunion at commencement week with the cus-
tomary Yale-Harvard baseball game, brass-band-led parades
from campus to the athletic field, and other Ivy League revelry.

But on June 26, 1900, as his classmates stepped off the train
to celebrate, Clifford Beers was laid up in Grace Hospital, having three days before fallen thirty feet from a ledge of his parents' Trumbull Street home. In fact, his whole family was at
dinner when his mother looked through a window to see her
son's body plummet past her and hit the ground. During the
week before his attempted suicide, Clifford Beers had been
seized by the most terrible dread that he might succumb to the
epileptic seizures that had wracked—and then killed—his
younger brother. He had also found himself examining his entire family history, which proved troublingly full of instability
and eccentricity. His four siblings all had serious emotional or
neurological disorders; all the Beers children but Clifford
would eventually die in mental hospitals—two by suicide.
There were other black marks on the Beers family tree, nearly
all of them cases of insanity.

In the week leading up to the Triennial, Clifford—popular
with his classmates, he had been elected to the Planning
Committee—hatched a dozen plans to end his own life: rowing

out to Lake Whitney to drown himself; swallowing a deadly dose of some poison; cutting his throat with a razor. His increasing dread left him sleepless, and finally, on June 23, he determined to throw himself from his room on the fourth floor of his parents' home. As had recurred often throughout his life, a cacophony of voices wracked his mind, which "felt as if pricked by a million needles at white heat."

His mother had just offered him dessert; in the three-minute interval while she fetched the pie from the kitchen, Clifford rushed to the fourth floor, climbed out on the window ledge, and then hurled himself toward the flagstone walk below. Missing the stone pavement by inches and hitting soft earth, he crushed one heel bone and almost all the small bones in the arches of both feet. For six years the demoniacal voices had tortured him. The instant he struck the ground, they were gone.

But new tortures awaited him that week while recuperating from his fall.

He imagined that the hot poultices applied by the hospital nurses were some "third degree" sweating ordeal designed to extract a confession. Now in place of the voices there were was a hellish vocal hum. Ghostly rappings on the walls and ceiling of his room were punctuated by unintelligible mumblings of invisible persecutors. He had a hallucination that he was trapped aboard a sinking ocean steamship; as it sank, he devised an electric tram system to spirit the passengers to safety. Each car that passed his hospital window was instantly translated into a vision of a trolley car on the phantom ship's deck.

As the Triennial celebrants arrived, Clifford was seized by the conviction that they intended to grab him from his hospital

bed, drag him to the athletic field lawn, and there tear him limb
from limb. In his words: "The college cries which filled the air
that afternoon struck more terror to my heart than all the Yale
cheers of history have struck to the hearts of vanquished rivals
on field or water." Six years after his waking nightmare, Clifford
Beers, having chronicled his episode of madness in *A Mind
That Found Itself* (1908), sent the manuscript to Professor William James at Harvard. James had struggled mightily with his
own depression and thoughts of suicide, and was deeply appre-
ciative of the "style and temper" of Beers's account:

> The most striking thing in it to my mind is the sudden conver-
> sion of you from a delusional subject to a maniacal one—how
> the whole delusional system disintegrated the moment one pin
> was drawn out by your proving your brother to be genuine. I
> never heard of so rapid a change in a mental system.

Responding to Beers's inquiry to James as to how he might
improve the book, William James replied: "Don't you do it. You
can hardly improve your book." In 1908, when Longmans,
Green & Company published the book, it prefaced it with
James's salutatory letter to Beers.

A Mind That Found Itself achieved considerable notoriety,
for Beers painted a grim portrait of the three institutions where
he received treatment, including Dr. Amos J. Givens's Sanitarium for the Treatment of Nervous and Mental Diseases, Opium
and Alcoholic Habitués at Stamford. Beers described how, as
his parents drove him to the New Haven station on a hot August day, he imagined all the shuttered houses as having been

deserted by their inhabitants to express their displeasure with him. Pulling into Stamford, when he saw workmen lounging in front of their factory reading newspapers on a break, Beers believed the papers to contain an account of his crimes. He believed every single person seen through the train window knew who and what he was. Catching sight of a Yale classmate, Beers was sure that the man was there to let him know that Yale was one of the powers behind the torture chamber to which he was now assigned.

In exacting detail, Clifford Beers reported each paranoid fantasy he suffered while at the Stamford sanitorium. He then chronicled the same for his stay at the Hartford Hospital for the Insane and one other institution. For all three, he provided a devastating account of the neglect and abuse he had suffered at the hands of attendants. Building on the success of his book in raising public awareness of the arbitrary cruelty inflicted on inmates of psychiatric institutions, Beers went on to found the Connecticut Society for Mental Hygiene, and in 1913 also founded the Clifford Beers Clinic in New Haven—the first outpatient mental health clinic in the United States. He remained a leader in the field until his retirement in 1939.

Dr. Givens's sanitorium, in 1900 about two miles north of the train station, was described by Beers as "situated in the country." From 1969 until 1996 it was home to the Olin Corporation; the poison-spewing Olin was one of the first companies to create a corporate campus in Stamford, so as to be close to its executives' homes. Today its buildings have been repurposed to serve as home to Gen Re—whose poisonous and fraudulent reinsurance scams have cost it as little in court-imposed penalties as Olin paid for its trail of spoiled landscapes and lives.

It would have been only about a half hour's walk from Stamford Town Center, where I was scheduled for a six-thirty p.m. performance of *Captain of a Huckleberry Party* at the Barnes & Noble, to 120 Long Ridge Road. I was keen to see what sort of use Olin and Gen Re had made of the previous healing campus grounds of Dr. Givens's sanitorium. Arriving in Stamford mid-afternoon, I had plenty of time to make the walk, but the downtown—particularly the Town Center mall—deadened my curiosity and initiative. I'd make my pedestrian presence known right there on Greyrock Place, which had been a village-green-like place where Atlantic, Pacific, and Canal Streets had converged when Clifford Beers arrived for his rehabilitation in August 1900. Village green no more; less than two thousand feet from the present Amtrak station, it is absolutely impossible to go as the crow flies, for the interstate and the Purdue Pharma and BTG Pactual bunkers stand like gargantuans threatening Nurse Ratched.

By the time I had found my way into the Stamford Town Center, I felt like Chief Bromden after the electroshock treatments. I circled the building, looking in vain for some sign of a bookstore. I asked a couple of skateboarders, but they had no clue. Finally, having walked one and a half times around the million-square-foot monstrosity's perimeter, I found a uniform-clad middle school student headed there to get a book she needed for a school project. As she led me through a corridor that could have been the entrance to a missile silo or penitentiary, we came upon two other pairs of confused shoppers.

They had just barely gotten out of their cars and were already lost.

As 6:30 p.m. neared, there were perhaps a dozen patrons in the enormous two-story Barnes & Noble store. At 6:25, a trim, handsome man with copper skin approached me, introduced himself as "Mazen," and asked if I was the fellow who wrote the book about Henry Thoreau.

"I was so excited when I saw the sign yesterday at the entrance to the store," he told me. "When I was in college in Damascus in the 1970s, I saw a performance of *The Night Thoreau Spent in Jail*—in Arabic—and that got me interested in Thoreau, Emerson, and the other transcendentalists."

Speaking further with Mazen, I learned that he had been studying to be a filmmaker, but after college, having gone to work for a hotel, he was drawn into the world of hotel management, and rose through the ranks at Marriott. Having arrived in Stamford with his family as a refugee from Syria—by way of a twenty-year stay in London—only five months before, he was still adjusting to his new life.

With Mazen sitting alone in the front row, I recited a trio of Thoreau's poems, in the form of a riddle, and then went on with my presentation. Occasionally a store patron would pass close to the back row of chairs, and I'd stop and try to lure them over, but no one accepted my invitation. Then, about halfway through my performance, a second person came straight up the center aisle, picked up one of the books on the table, opened it, and then put it back down.

I beckoned. "Hello, please join us. Are you interested in Henry David Thoreau?"

"I'm not sure," she replied. "I don't wish to speak. I have no teeth."

I felt it would be pleasant company for Mazen if I could get her to stay, so I persevered. "What's your name?"

"Eva. From Lithuania."

"Ah, wonderful. Mazen is from Syria. Henry and I have a very international audience tonight."

I continued, and a moment later Eva rose and walked away, leaving me, Henry, and Mazen in a most intimate exchange, an odd but beautiful and poignant dance, given what Mazen's nation was at that moment suffering thanks to the mad machinations of my nation, and Henry's.

❧

HENRY SAID ABOUT Hugh Quoil that "he died in the road," a seemingly innocent enough expression to our twenty-first century ears, but one that carried with it in Henry's time the most shameful, tragic implications and connotations. It suggested the epitome of abandonment and ostracism from one's fellow humanity. What might this poor Irishman, whom Henry described as a "man of manners," "capable of more civil speech than you could well attend to," have done to leave him alone and abandoned at death? In the passage in *Walden*, Henry says, almost in passing, how Hugh's garden had not been tilled, "owing to those terrible shaking fits."

As luck would have it, a Stamford psychiatrist named Percy R. Vessie, the medical director at the Stamford Sanitarium for three decades after Clifford Beers's sojourn there, had ensured that I could not read that phrase without wondering if Hugh Quoil had perhaps been afflicted with Huntington's disease. In 1932, when Vessie published his paper "On the Transmission of Huntington's Chorea for 300 Years: The Bures Family Group" in the *Journal of Nervous and Mental Disease*, he referred to the disease by its older name, Huntington's *chorea*, a Greek word meaning "dance," as in "St. Vitus's dance," the term that had prevailed for centuries before East Hampton physician George Huntington had in 1872 written the classic description, based on long experience with the debilitating disease among a number of East Hampton families.

Starting with one of his own patients, Vessie constructed a pedigree chart that traced the origin of the disease back to three men who had immigrated to New England from the East Anglia town of Bures, in Suffolk, in the 1630s. Through twelve generations, Vessie mapped this "horrible heredity" by way of black ("Chorea") and x-hatched ("Chorea not verified") circles (females) and squares (males), and other circles signifying "Witch" and squares marked "Misconduct." Vessie alleged that these immigrants' social pathology and acts of delinquency—documented, he said, in colonial court proceedings—signaled that they may have suffered from Huntington's chorea. Thieves, quacks, and lawbreakers, they were "notorious principals in unsavory colonial history," who had been "illiterate and arrogant." None "attained recognition or respectability," declared the Stamford psychiatrist turned medical historian. Their descendants were conspicuous for their "spitefulness, bickering, querulousness and blasphemy," and the pity they would normally expect to receive was understandably denied them due to their bizarre dancelike movements and "cantankerous behavior."

What especially caught Vessie's imagination was the possibility that the Bures men's wives—specifically one "Ellin Nichols" (following eugenic family study protocol, Vessie gave the individuals fictional names)—had been witches. "We believe," Vessie asserted, "the true story of this lesion to be revealed in the witchcraft trials of women in the Bures group." The only way to prevent this disorderly, disgusting disease of mind and body from spreading in Stamford and elsewhere was "rigid sterilization." This radical surgical intervention in people's reproductive lives would surely stem "the sorrowful march of victims to the scaffold, exile and social ostracism."

Vessie's sensationalized, almost wholly fictive tale linking witches and ne'er-do-wells with Huntington's chorea shaped both the clinical practice of generations of American physicians and the research programs of scientists. From the stories of disabled neighbors seeking his medical help, Vessie wove a horrific medical narrative that cursed the self-images of afflicted families for generations. The symmetry with the *Linguistic Atlas*'s encounter with the "mean old rich man of Stamford" is chilling. A story, set in stone, taints and terrifies "even unto the seventh generation." But the story is a cruel fiction, a product not of observation and experience, but of small-minded fears and prejudices and misunderstandings across social and cultural boundaries. In the era of vengeful, stupid Trumpism, we would do well to scrutinize and share Stamford's saga of this ill-boded "dance."

I knew this story well before I arrived in Stamford, for

thirty-five years earlier I had stumbled on the records of the Eugenics Survey of Vermont, in the old laundry building of the Vermont State Hospital in Waterbury. Of the dozens of pedigree charts—some as long as six feet!—in the documents there, Pedigree #1 was the "Chorea Family," a Vermont version of Vessie's horror story, and equally fictional. Though researchers had as early as 1969 documented the multiple errors in Vessie's genealogies, respected physicians and medical researchers continued to perpetuate Vessie's myth right up to the early twenty-first century. When Alice Wexler, whose own family suffered from Huntington's disease, published *The Woman Who Walked Into the Sea* in 2007, she not only exposed Vessie's and others' pernicious mistruths, but also offered an extraordinary story of how, in the "type location" of Huntington's chorea, East Hampton, Long Island, the community had for generations, from the early seventeenth century right up to the time of Huntington's medical case study, adapted itself in creative and compassionate ways to the individuals who suffered the spasms and sorrows of this mysterious malady.

Phebe Hedges, the wife of East Hampton farmer and selectman "Captain" David Hedges, walked into the sea in June 1806 because of her dread of the disorder then still called St. Vitus's dance. Alice Wexler almost miraculously discovered that Phebe Hedges's tragic fate had been, like those of countless other souls throughout history, directed by the judgmental ways of her neighbors. Phebe had walked into the sea shortly after her beloved husband had been nearly fatally crushed by his own horses and wagon, in the wake of the advancing deadly illness of her mother, and in a moment when she was deeply troubled about changes she noticed in herself. The celebrated Presbyterian preacher Lyman Beecher had on New Year's Day 1806 delivered a jeremiad disguised as a "General History of the Town of East Hampton." The once-blessed village, Reverend Beecher instructed his congregation, had ransomed its "glorious inheritance," degenerating into an assortment of ills and errors that Providence had rewarded with suitably painful reckonings.

In the weeks leading up to her suicide, Phebe was ably and expertly attended to by Dr. Abel Huntington, who gave her spirits of turpentine, a stimulant, when her spirits were alarmingly low, and he also prescribed chamomile tonics, a common remedy for spasms. It was Dr. Huntington who was called away on June 18 to Montauk, where Phebe's body was found washed up on the beach. The obituary in the *Suffolk Gazette* did not report Phebe Hedges's suicide as an act of insanity or a crime or a lamentable lapse of giving in to temptation, but as the result of "melancholy" precipitated by her fear of St. Vitus's dance. Her "unfortunate" death was neither criminal nor crazy, but an act of fate wholly worthy of compassion and careful consideration.

Henry's perennial motto—"In the long run we find what we expect; we shall be fortunate, then, if we expect great things"— is a call not just to personal self-will, but to *selfless* will, to the highest striving for the benefit of *others*, not oneself. The places in both Henry's and our own times that seem particularly blessed are those where stories of good works, of the Golden Rule, of boundary-crossing in the service of others less fortunate, are the common coin of the realm. Stamford is not *yet* such a place. Maybe a hundred Mazens, "foreigners" filled with youthful ideals, can still make it so.

Dance out ignorance. Dance out superstition. Dance tyranny into oblivion. Others before us have done it, and so must we. Waltz, or jig, or jitterbug, the dances we do must make us *free*, not bind us. They should set in motion the spirit of Saint Paul: "Not I, but Christ in me." A student of Saint Paul, Saint Augustine, once said:

#3: Learn to DANCE, else the Angels won't know what to do with you.

CHAPTER 4

Into the Vortex: CREATE!

A WEEK BEFORE I began my walk, I went to get my hair cut. Vera had cut my hair once before, but we'd not spoken much on that visit. Full of expectation about my upcoming pilgrimage, on this day I was chatty, and so was Vera. I asked her about her life in St. Petersburg before she came to Brooklyn, and how she had met her husband, and she spoke freely about her twelve-year-old son, and her twin, who had married a rich oligarch back home. Anxious that Vera might share the intense conservatism and easy "patriotism" of my Brooklyn expatriate Slavic neighbors, I gingerly asked her opinion of Vladimir Putin.

Vera grew immediately animated, snipping away with her scissors faster and faster as she spoke with respect and even love for the Russian president. I replied by telling her about having grown up during the Cold War with a bomb shelter in our basement, and about *The Russians Are Coming!* paranoia with none of that 1966 film's humorous parody of American fear-mongering. She touched my right hand, turned it over, and said: "You always come back to places. You go far away, then you come back." Vera then proceeded for the next twenty minutes to inspect every line and crevice in my hand, pronouncing a series of the most extraordinarily accurate summations of some of the main leitmotifs of my life.

I thought of Vera as I came to Mill Plain Road in Fairfield, Connecticut. Turning north off the Post Road, a cascade of memories upon seeing the Exit 21 off-ramp of I-95. Every Sunday afternoon or evening in the summer of 1975, I had walked down that off-ramp, at the end of the long hitchhiking journey back from Woodstock, Vermont. I'd had the good fortune to land my dream summer job after my freshman year of college, working as an environmental education instructor for the Mill River ranger program, founded by a passionate educator and activist, Jocelyn "Joy" Shaw. When my parents had dropped me off at Mrs. Shaw's home—a converted eighteenth century gristmill on the south bank of the Mill River—we had come down that same ramp, in the old Ford Country Squire station wagon that had chauffeured me and my brother and sister to a thousand baseball games and doctors' visits and Dairy Queen runs.

We had turned onto Mill Plain Road too, and then, just beyond the Mill Plain Green (which looked exactly as it looked when I was nineteen), we veered off left onto Old Mill Road, then turned into Mrs. Shaw's driveway where Old Mill Road did a hairpin to parallel the river.

The mill pond outside Mrs. Shaw's door was not Walden

Pond, and my third-floor garret bedroom was not Henry's pine cabin, but that summer, just one summer after I'd first read *Walden*, was, in Henry's words, an "ambrosial" season, full of discovery and delight. Mentored by Mrs. Shaw, I explored the banks and bottom of the Mill River with a crazy cohort of junior counselors and a couple of dozen young "rangers" sporting a laughing kingfisher on their Mill River Wetland T-shirts. From the headwaters to the mouth at the Long Island Sound, we poked about in boats, slogged in sneakers, plumbed peat bogs with brass coring rods, conducted pH tests, and caught crayfish and blue crabs as they scuttled along the pebbly bottom of this middling river of the New England coast.

I had been blessedly riparian from birth, for after I was born on Manhattan Isle my parents carried me back to the bank of Ramsey Brook, a tiny tributary of the Saddle River, which joined the Passaic River five miles below the Passaic Falls at Paterson, New Jersey. That eight-foot-wide brook was completely crossable at all points, but for the time of spring floods, when it would fill our basement and send my mother to meet me and my brother and sister after school at the bridge to hold her hand, lest the floodwaters carry us away to the Hackensack Meadowlands. Indeed, our little brook was *jumpable*, its soft banks easily receiving our bodies after a flying leap across its narrow spots.

Stocked full of minnows, crayfish, carp, hellgrammites and water striders, musk turtles and soft-shells and snappers, and the biggest bullfrogs in North America by our estimation, Ramsey Brook was enough Walden Pond for us until we turned thirteen or fourteen, when, if we had become serious fishermen, we sought cleaner waters. But in 1960s America, for most of us,

teenhood meant shedding our riparian childhoods for the as-
phalt and lawns and organized activities of parks and athletic
fields. That halcyon summer apprenticing to Joy Shaw, I got an
invitation back to another brook, to catch crayfish and collect
caddis fly larvae, which we merrily peeled like bananas of their
pine-needle or sand-grain envelopes. Thank heavens I'd learned
to catch crayfish as a kid; nineteen was too late to teach even a
nimble shortstop the lightning-quick underwater maneuver to
pluck the wily backward-propelled marine crustacean in mid-
explosion.

Walking to see Mrs. Shaw perhaps twenty-five years since I
had last seen her, I knew I was her peer now, not her protégé
and amanuensis. Still, I was so full of questions. What books
had she assigned to me that summer to prepare for the task? I
recalled Luna Leopold's little *Water* primer and Marie Morisawa's *Streams: Their Dynamics and Morphology* (1968); I could
swear "dynamic" had entered my vocabulary that summer, as
Mrs. Shaw, with her cultivated Chapin School accent and her
blinking blue eyes, pronounced the word as a magical incanta-
tion, her oversized hands always out in front before her as she
spoke it, lightly clasping each other, then rotating like a lotus
flower set spinning, or a 3-D yin-yang of the hands.

That summer, in the tight, hermetic quarters of the old mill's
attic bedroom, I read Victor Hugo's *Les Misérables*, and there
are today etched into my soul so many scenes from Hugo's masterpiece. But these pale considered alongside the point bars,
meanders, cut banks, shallows, and deeps of the Mill River, as
it came rushing into my consciousness aided by Mrs. Shaw's
and Leopold's and Marie Morisawa's wisdom. Approaching the

hairpin on foot now, I could see that the river was about to spill it's banks, and this is exactly how my mind felt that summer. Turning into the driveway, I had but one image, from one of the first days out with the rangers. Upriver a short distance where the town of Fairfield stored its gravel and salt for winter road-work, we had mounted a tall gravel pile with big five-gallon compound buckets half full of water dipped from the river. At Mrs. Shaw's signal, we had emptied, one after another, our buckets in the same gravel spot, and then watched the sped-up geomorphological microcosm of river formation. Braided chan-nels, meanders, even an oxbow formed out of nowhere. The kids—me included—were transfixed. That whole summer, as we netted minnows or examined litmus paper or laid out the papery husks of dragonfly and damselfly nymphs, we went back in memory to our sand-and-gravel play of that first day, full of wonder that an inorganic channel in clay and sand and gravel could be turned into such a prodigious nursery for life.

Perhaps the most famous passage in *Walden* is Henry's oper-atic description of the sand-and-clay bank of the railroad's "Deep Cut" along Walden Pond's western shore. It is a master-piece of metamorphism—both metamorphic subject and ob-ject, description and described. In Henry's hands, the two fuse ecstatically, and in so doing the macrocosm seeps in, inspiring Henry to ask: "Who knows what the human body would ex-pand and flow out to under a more genial heaven?

"Thus," Henry concludes after turning all the Earth into a branching hieroglyph of Heaven, "it seemed that this one hill-side illustrated all the operations of Nature." It was just this im-plicit truth, this all-encompassing emblematic, that had seized

us on our sandbank on the Mill River's margin. That we had
stood atop the mound and set it in motion made this truth eve
more powerful. Coming to Mrs. Shaw's side door, peeking in
see her ancient teakettle on the stovetop rocking side to s
silent due to a cracked whistle topknot, for a fleeting ins
felt that I too, like Henry, had touched the heart of Crea
and found there not some dangerous Promethean power, b
playful dance. The big revelation of our gravel bank was th
flowing water corkscrewed amid its containing banks of whatever size, and so it was a living thing, spiraling both hidden and
invisible materials into its vortical self. Now, at the threshold of
that 1975 summer once more, it was as if I had just discovered
my own biography's Rosetta stone, for the vortex was a template, an arcanum, and an attractor of a wide watershed of mysteries into my life.

Decades before modernist British artist and writer Wynd-
ham Lewis declared—in 1914—"Long Live the Vortex!" as an
artistic call to arms, a variety of nineteenth century sciences
discovered and celebrated the vortex, finding it spectacularly
expressed at both the microcosmic and macrocosmic ends of
the visible universe. In 1840, New York City steamship entre-
preneur William C. Redfield showed that tornadoes—as well as
larger, less destructive atmospheric movements—had a vortical
form. In 1858, American geologist William B. Rogers described
his experiments on the formation of vortices in air and liquids,
only months after Hermann von Helmholtz published a paper
("On Integrals of the Hydrodynamic Equations That Corre-
spond to Vortex Motions") that translated the vortex into a
mathematical equation. In 1861, James Clerk Maxwell would

rest his electromagnetic theory upon a vortical basis; in 1869, Lord Kelvin (almost two decades after his brother, James, had patented a vortex turbine for a British paper mill) published his vortex atom theory; in 1875, Lord Kelvin's smoke-ring-studying friend Peter Guthrie Tait teamed up with Balfour Stewart to write *The Unseen Universe*, an attempt at a unified theory of science and religion, with the vortex as its central motif; in 1884, Cavendish Professor of Experimental Physics at Cambridge University J. J. Thomson won the Adams Prize for his *Treatise on the Motion of Vortex Rings*; in 1908, astronomer George Ellery Hale made the first photographs of sunspots, showing them to be vortices. That same year, James Bell Pettigrew's posthumous three-volume masterpiece, *Design in Nature*, described and portrayed vortical forms from galaxies to the musculature of the human heart.

All of these scientific developments testify both to the era's spectacular expansion of visionary capacity into the physical world and to Western science's proclivity for modeling. In the case of Hale's sunspots or Isaac Roberts's pioneering photographs of spiral nebulae (aka "galaxies"), the human eye was for the first time seeing the macrocosmic manifestations of the vortical form; at the microcosmic level, physicists were merely *imagining* vortical forms and motions, but constantly mistaking their models for reality. The vortex model-as-reality error was not confined to materialist thinkers: with seemingly all of literate Western culture entranced by Kelvin's vortex atom, mesmeric physician Edwin D. Babbitt's 1878 *Principles of Light and Color* mixed John Ruskin's aesthetics, Baron Karl von Reichenbach's odylism, and his own fanatical rage for system to produce a mesmero-spiritualist study of the "finer forces." A considerable portion of the book was devoted to building up an abstract, totally speculative model of the atom. Babbitt's drawing of his fantasy atom—with its legend of "VORTEX" prominent at the top center—yet lives, in dozens of forms, thanks to Annie Besant and C. W. Leadbeater's *Occult Chemistry* (1908), which reproduced Babbitt's invention as a clairvoyant perception of the *anu*, or "occult atom."

At the very same moment when materialist science was creating mental models of nature as vortex, H. P. Blavatsky—in both her 1877 work *Isis Unveiled* and more extensively in *The Secret Doctrine* (1885)—affirmed the occult foundation of knowledge about the vortical dimension of cosmogenesis. She gives the fifth "Stanza of Dzyan" in Volume I of *The Secret Doctrine*:

> "Wheels" . . . are the centers of force, around which primordial cosmic matter expands, and passing through all the six stages of consolidation, becomes spheroidal and ends by being transformed into spheres or globes. It is one of the fundamental dogmas of Esoteric cosmogony, that during the *kalpas* (or Aeons) of life, motion, which, during the periods of rest, pulsates and thrills through every slumbering atom—assumes an ever growing tendency to circular movement. "The Deity becomes a Whirlwind."

Madame Blavatsky suggested that the law of vortical movement was a nearly universal occult precept, known both to initiates of ancient Greek mysteries and to the modern clairvoyant

Swedish natural scientist Emanuel Swedenborg. The British Christian esotericist C. G. Harrison, in lectures in London in 1893, gave as the ultimate of his "Three Great Axioms," "All Phenomena have their Origin in Vortices"—and in 1904, German esotericist Rudolf Steiner went beyond both Blavatsky and Harrison to proclaim that "the human being must become a Vortex." All of these esotericists—all of whom one might term "transcendentalists"—were speaking of forms and forces beyond the material.

It was a truly corkscrewed path that carried me from that summer of 1975, and dreams of happily inhabiting a Thoreauvian persona in late twentieth century America, to waters deeper and murkier than any of the Mill River's, or even than the waters of Long Island Sound or indeed the continental shelf beyond. You make a road or river your own, not by conquest or by design, but by rhythm. The rhythm Vera had caught in my aura, and expressed somehow in the irregular rhythm of wrinkles in my right hand, was the rhythm of *return*. I was arriving now at Mrs. Shaw's back door sure that the form to which she had introduced me—the vortex—was the arcanum of arcana, even more fundamental than Henry's insight that "The Maker of this earth but patented a leaf."

Turn, if you will, from the spongy shores of Walden Pond and the Mill River to Arcanum XVII of the tarot—the Star. The woman kneeling there on the riverbank, one foot in the water, the other upon the earth, pours water from jugs in both hands. She could be one of the Mill River rangers, intent on creating something dynamic, living, *growing*. A tower is built; a tree grows. On this walk I'd passed the premier towers of the last century, from the Park Row Building's twin copper cupolas—tallest in the world in 1899—to F. W. Woolworth's Cathedral of Commerce across Broadway, which surpassed its neighbor as tallest in the world in 1916; and World Trade Center One, looming up above the Woolworth Building like a bird of prey; and the sad towers of Stamford, which obscure—for a moment—the old town's noble steeples. There are, flanking the flowing-haired goddess of Arcanum XVII, a pair of luxuriant trees. Those two trees are all trees and every tree, needing no engraved cornerstone; no bronze plaque with the name of the architect and builder embossed upon it; no title. A tower is built (by man); a tree grows (by God).

Stick, my friend, like this arcanum's goddess, to the river, for there you will find the most plentiful and dynamic pictures of the living landscape, the spiral growth in its myriad manifestations. A whole microscopic world of unicellular water animals—the infusoria—incorporate the archetypal spiraling movement of water into their form, and they propel themselves screwlike through their watery home. The algae's translucent shoots; the frosted elfin, hoary edge skipper, and wild indigo duskywing chrysalids clinging to wild indigo; the bitty beans inside the black indigo pods; all have and are organs of vortical extra-vagance. The ostrich fern's unfurling fiddleheads; the snail's humble Golden Section; fish scales and fish bones. Hang about at the river's edge, collect the beach wrack, and you will find the flotsam and jetsam, the carcasses of the vortex of life.

Kneel on the bank and pull up and inspect those jellied egg masses of wood frogs and spotted salamanders, and see how as soon as the fertilized egg breaks free of the circular form, it becomes one spiraling half of the Tao. Imagine the tarot card's water bearer with child, then contemplate the polonaise inside her womb. Beyond the resolution of your hand lens, vortical miracles are happening by the second. A sphere deforms into an irregular ellipsoid, morphing as its surface increases faster than its volume. Cell membrane and nucleus, kinetically bound to each other by shared cytoplasm, push, pull. The membrane's submicroscopic molecules migrate into the nucleus's alchemical alembic, then circle back to the elastic boundary.

Waves flow in and out. Designs appear and disappear. We call them "blastula," "morula," "blastocyst," and such, but biology's terms for the phases of this miracle that is the embryo obscure more than they reveal; there really are no "phases," no pauses, just the seamless simmering of that wholly invisible fuse that births form after form.

But in all vertebrates, from frog and salamander to human being, there comes a moment when a thin line of lateral ectodermal cells splits off and migrates along the surface. Gaining mass and momentum, it scores a seam down its own axis. On either side, swirls of cells send themselves centerwise in a looping arc, vanishing into a crevice christened the "primitive streak." This opens into a groove, then a gash; the cells surge forward, plunging into the embryo's core. Then one sees the vortex . . . Arrested here, on the threshold of gastrulation, the little embryo resembles a larval jellyfish that could trade this uterine sanctuary for the sea.

Vertebrates both above and below the frog and salamander on up to us unfold from embryo to adult in this eternal polonaise. It is God's music, God's dance, God's way of growth, though for fear of its misuse by the pinnacles of Her/His creation, that way has for millennia been imparted only in the cryptic language of hermeticism, or stripped of its essence by the language of materialist natural science.

At the physical level of reality, the human being—swirling about embryonically as the polonaise movement—begins life as a vortex, a lemniscate. The highest initiates in all places and times have said that we must "end" as a vortex too; that is, to incorporate into ourselves the very growth powers of the Creator, to become Creators ourselves. God's promise is that we turn ourselves and the Earth inside out, transforming both bodies into radiant, life-giving, ever-increasing *suns*. Like the river cutting into one bank, then corkscrewing on to another point in our biography where we lay down new material for exploration and discovery, our lives pulse between creation and destruction.

Sitting with Mrs. Shaw that afternoon in the central room whose big window looks out onto the mill pond, we compare more notes than there have been years between our last visit, and as we speak, my gratitude for her mentorship grows like skunk cabbage or witch hazel or willow—those select few of so many riparian plants whose powers of growth exceed their less liquid cousins. The hour is getting late; I wish for some apotheosis to present itself, lest we spill like the river over our own banks.

"May I show you something?"

"Of course."

Facing Mrs. Shaw and the river, I step forward with my right foot, and, as I do so, spread my arms and sweep them toward the floor, rocking gently forward. As I bring them up, fingertips nearly touching, until they have come to the top of the arc above my head, I rock back. Arms and hands parting into two complementary whorls, I rock forward again.

"This is the *L*—the Aquarius sound, and its gesture of an eternal flowing fountain. It seemed the proper way to say goodbye, until next time."

The dance keeps me from saying more than I know. It wakes the angels to me, and I to them, and it makes Mrs. Shaw—this dynamic, dynamite eighty-six-year-old woman whose very own gestures catch the vortex's green and irrepressible fuse—very happy.

#4: Become a Vortex—CREATE!

CHAPTER 5

Captaining Huckleberry Parties: SENSE!

I F YOU WOULD KNOW the flavor of huckleberries," Henry wryly declared, "ask the cowboy or the partridge." Or ask Henry himself. The original connoisseur of terroir, he didn't need to ask cowboy or partridge, as he had plucked ripe and underripe and very probably overripe fruit from these altogether everyday shrubs from Sudbury Meadow to Yellow Birch Swamp, the Bedford Levels to Annursnac Hill—all four corners of Concord. While his botanist contemporaries went about furiously splitting the genus *Gaylussacia* into dozens and dozens of species, all based on microscopic and highly plastic physical characteristics of leaves and flowers, Henry practiced more sublime speciation studies, hewing to huckleberry's "ambrosial" qualities of taste and texture and poetic tendencies.

Emerson's moniker "Captain of a Huckleberry Party," if a little cruel, was also accurate, for there was about the annual ritual of gathering the prosaic fruit a distinct atmosphere of carnival, a frugivorous charivari; and what are carnivals and charivari if not invitations to open one's senses wide?

Henry was a rank sensualist, more Whitmanesque than Whitman in his delight in the multitudes—not of human form and urban activity, but of the ways in which one could use mouth, nose, ears, eyes, and skin to discern and delight in one's sensual surround. He was a true friend of Eros, whose forgotten forté is always and everywhere the unfettered *giving away* with each and every in-breath of sensory awareness. Henry made his sensing a prayer, and so, dear reader, can we, especially at this moment when digital devices threaten to usurp our sensing as well as our thinking capacities.

On a long walk, one's senses open slowly but steadily, like the fern fronds and jack-in-the-pulpit spathes that started to stir in the Connecticut oak and hickory woods as I made my way to New Haven. I was disappointed to know that though Emerson had lectured there a few times, Henry had not, so there would be no local shrine to seek out. Other themes and questions would need to present themselves.

As it so happened, in the weeks leading up to the pilgrimage, I had been working on a pair of inquiries—about peneplains and pterodactyls—that fit perfectly with a sojourn New Haven-way. The first was a quest to understand my own early physiographic proclivities, the second a small sideline inquiry for an epic book about evolution. They converged nicely at New Haven, for the old Puritan town was the home and research epicenter of America's most prolific natural scientist, James Dwight Dana. I was keen to see Dana's home, and since it was now the

Yale Department of Statistics and Data Science, that seemed eminently possible to do.

Before immersing myself in the handsome architecture of the Yale campus, I wanted to get a bird's-eye view of the burgh from the top of West Rock, Dana's favorite Triassic-era igneous intrusion into that region's "country rock"—the ubiquitous red sandstone of the Connecticut Valley. Before this walk to West Rock, I read Dana's 1870 *On the Geology of the New Haven Region*. I had enjoyed Professor Dana's voice many years before, as I hunted up geographical and geological arcana of New England in the *American Journal of Science*—which Dana edited for almost fifty years from his Hillhouse Avenue home. Just bringing the acronym *AJS* to mind made my whole body ring with memory, of the yellowed, often spotted pages of the journal; of the gorgeous marbled endpapers; the myriad voices of America's most curious "sensors" of the landscape. Though Henry Thoreau never contributed to the *AJS*, he was a faithful and interested spectator of its cabinet of wonders.

Along with the faint images of the quaint woodcut illustrations that liberally decorated the journal's pages, I had hundreds of inner impressions, pictures made by my imagination as I read it thirty years ago. In my years of perusing the *American Journal of Science*, I'd never come to know Dana in his habitat. He was the center of the wide network of collecting and describing of the North American continent, and it had totally escaped my notice that the *AJS* editor and author of the unrivaled nineteenth century textbook on geology, Dana's *Manual of Geology* (1863), lived at a critical point on the compass of American

natural history description. The New Haven hinterland was a
prime place of geological discovery and theorizing. The feature
that made it so attractive was that the ancient Paleozoic rocks of
the region were gracefully bisected by New England's heartland
river—the Connecticut, or "Long," River. As Dana understood
Earth history here, the formation of the Connecticut was one of
the last events of the Paleozoic, precipitated by the bending of
the Earth's crust, as a sequel to the crystallization of the granite,
gneiss, crystalline schists, and other rocks that constituted the
bottom of the valley.

Prehistoric, Paleozoic New Haven was the southern termi-
nus of a twenty-mile-wide estuary that stretched to northern
Massachusetts, into which Dana, and all his contemporaries
and all geological thinkers since, imagined to have existed at
the edge of a great ancient ocean 250 million years ago. There
was a beautiful, nested symmetry here, as spectacular an expression of James Hutton and Charles Lyell's uniformitarianism (the processes that we can now see have *always* prevailed)
as anywhere in North America, that laid one still-quivering
Quaternary estuary upon a petrified Paleozoic one. The deep
logic of these landscape features impressed itself upon anyone
who cared to look. That landscape had clearly broken into
"blocks" that were either thrown up or dropped down, then
were incised by rivers. The pièce de resistance was glaciation;
much of what Dana and his neighbors looked upon had been
stripped bare by the glacier.

In New Haven's capacious harbor, one could observe the
continuities of geomorphology in the daily cycles of deposition
and erosion, the flow and ebb engine of all bedrock save the

igneous. That this was the landscape that gave birth to Harvard geographer William Morris Davis's theory of the "geographical cycle," a theory that prevailed from the 1890s into my own freshman geology course in 1975, was no accident.

There was much that I could not say to Mrs. Shaw about my post–Mill River ranger, post-Dartmouth, and post–University of Vermont master's degree in geography education that I wish, dear reader, without numbing your senses and mind, to say to you. The esoteric order into which I had stumbled, or, more properly, into which my angel had led me, was an even more cryptic and conspiratorial one than Skull and Bones, though it had no crypts or secret oaths or handshakes. Walking with Henry—whose geological and paleontological pictures ran quite in parallel with James Dwight Dana's—into Professor Dana's town, nestled below the traprock intrusives of West and East Rock, I was carrying pictures that truly would have blown his mind, at least at first telling. I'd like to think that, given a chance, he might have come some way toward taking them in as his own.

In the decades when Henry was peering into deep time by studying the succession of trees in the Walden Woods and Dana was collecting rock samples from the face of West Rock, dinosaurs were not yet monster reptile stars; top billing went to ichthyosaurs and pterodactyls—known by the taxonomic term "pterosaurs" today. These strange beasts had dominated paleontological iconography ever since 1830, when English geologist Henry De la Beche featured them in *Duria Antiquior*, the first imaginative artistic depiction of a scene from the Mesozoic world. They still had monster cachet in 1922. That summer, at the Hotel McAlpin in Manhattan, Sir Arthur Conan Doyle had shown to his friend Harry Houdini and his fellow Society of American Magicians members a few minutes of a test reel of *The Lost World*, the feature-length film of Conan Doyle's bestselling 1912 novel. The finished film's first matchup of "prehistoric brutes" would show a stop-motion animation simulation of a pteranodon killing and eating a young toxodon—a Pleistocene mammal; in the brief footage the magicians saw half a dozen other prehistoric species battling each other.

In wedding the new technology of the motion picture to clay models of ancient animals, special effects designer Willis O'Brien certainly had pulled off an astonishing magic trick; even Houdini himself was baffled by what he saw. O'Brien and Conan Doyle fully believed in the accuracy of their miniature monsters, which were themselves modeled on museum reconstructions. Paleontology even in Dana's pre-cinema era obscured the degree to which it was a vast imaginative exercise; once animation came along, the public entered into the dreamworld of the scientists, believing their inventions to be real. Paleontology is really an epic sleight-of-hand, for no paleontologist has ever *seen* a pterodactyl or ichthyosaur or brontosaurus. The illusion of time travel has since Dana's day been the central conceit of all portraits of the Earth's early history. *Jurassic Park* is just a recent iteration of an old con.

℔

IN SEPTEMBER 1922, while speaking to a group of construction workers in Dornach, Switzerland, in a lecture titled "Early Conditions of the Earth," Rudolf Steiner painted vivid pictures of the ichthyosaur and its ancient environment. Steiner described ichthyosaurs as half swimming, half wading in a habitat of greenish-brown sludge, looking quite like the pre-Claymation characters of *The Lost World*—a dolphin-like head, with long jaws bearing large crocodile-like conical teeth, and front fins like those of a whale. He also emphasized their large eyes, but added that these eyes glowed like electric lights, and that above their heads they had another gigantic eye that acted like a lantern, shining into the distance.

Alongside the ichthyosaurs lived plesiosaurs, which had bodies like whales and heads like lizards and four stout legs. Above all, Steiner emphasized the "frightfully strong" ribs of the plesiosaurs, whom he called "lazy fellows," attributing their laziness to the fact that the Earth at that time rotated much more slowly than today. Illustrating the scene with colored chalk upon a blackboard, Steiner pictured both the lantern-bearing ichthyosaur and the chevron-ribbed plesiosaur, whose eyes he positioned more to the side of the head. Filling in with red chalk a zone just above them, and labeling it *Feuerluft* ("fire-mist"), he placed within it a single *Drachenvogel*—"dragon bird," his term for a pterosaur, and then described how the ichthyosaur used its luminous lantern organ to hypnotize the pterosaur, which then plunged out of the fire-mist into the muddy sludge environment (*Erdschlamm*) below.

Steiner's pterosaur description was even wilder than the one he gave for the ichthyosaur. Flying about on batlike wings that were acutely sensitive to the Sun and Moon, the pterosaurs formed a luminous electromagnetic sheath around themselves, such that out of their own forces they would "shine and glimmer like fireflies." When they stretched out their wings, they felt a wave of intense well-being, especially so under the stars, which they felt so keenly that the individual stars left impressions in their skin. Steiner told his audience of very practical, down-to-earth laborers that a close study of the fossil wing imprints of the pterosaur would show there to be "all kinds of stars" that had left impressions in the wings. He also claimed that because of their "electrical" nature, the pterosaurs caused the ichthyosaurs great abdominal pain. The pterosaurs, on the other hand, had a pleasurable sense when they were in the throat of an ichthyosaur! "Just as the Turks wanted to go to Paradise, these birds regarded it as their salvation to go down the throat of an Ichthyosaurus."

More astonishing still, the ichthyosaurs (and plesiosaurs), in digesting the pterosaurs, took on new forms: the ichthyosaur became the "*Seekuh*" (sea cow, or manatee, most likely *Prorastomus sirenoides*, a primitive sirenian from the Eocene, circa forty million years ago), and the plesiosaur became the "Megatherien" (the giant ground sloth, *Megatherium spp.*). As for pterosaurs, Steiner said that after they disappeared from the Earth, they later reappeared as eagles and vultures, preserving the pterosaurs' acute eyesight.

Each of these instances of radical transformation—pterosaur to birds of prey; ichthyosaur to manatees; plesiosaur to ground sloths—is not so much "speciation" as fantastic, unimaginable metamorphosis, for in all three cases the shift is at the taxonomic level of class—fully four ranks of biological classification above the species level. Reptiles (class Reptilia) become birds (class Aves) and mammals (class Mammalia)! With this single lecture, and explicit attention to but three Mesozoic animals, Rudolf Steiner threw wide open the question of how, during Earth history, animal forms changed. This is of course the central question of evolutionary biology. Steiner left unanswered a vast array of fundamental questions about morphological change over time, despite his sustained critique of Darwinian theory, as well as his offering—throughout his books and lectures—a vastly elaborated view of evolution emphasizing (1) the co-evolution of Earth and humanity; (2) the priority of spiritual involution in advance of physical evolution; and (3) the human being as the "stem" from which all animals originated.

Having been schooled since my dinosaur-loving youth in Darwinian pictures of the past, I found my jaw hanging at Rudolf Steiner's renegade paleontology, but by the time I walked with Henry into New Haven, *his* pictures had come to replace those upon which I had been raised. Even more fundamental than Steiner's heterodox portrait of metamorphic animal bodies was his picture of Earth as a plastic body as fully capable of metamorphosis as Mesozoic marine monsters. Before we were bones—from the tips of our toes and metatarsals to the top of our vaulted cranium—we were gelatin, albumen, aqueous vapor, a flicker of warmth enveloped by ice. Before we became Leonardo's Vitruvian Man—the length of our outspread arms equal to our height; the distance from our elbow to our armpit one-eighth our height; our face proportioned in perfect thirds from chin to nose to eyebrows to hairline; and the whole symphony of skeletal melodies consonant with the music of the spheres—we were ourselves a simple sphere, a single chaotic cell floating down our mother's fallopian tube toward the womb.

And before Earth was bone—basaltic gabbros and perido-
tites; granitic continental craton; crystalline schists interleaved
with mica and garnet and magnetite and marble; limestone,
shale, sandstone—it too was gelatin, albumen, aqueous vapor, a
warm hollow in ice. Before it spat out Sun and Moon—
simultaneous with the human standing upright, to gain memory before true consciousness—Earth was a living protoplasmic
colloid, within which archaebacteria birthed both the oxygen-
ated atmosphere and organic sulfur-nitrate-phosphorus and
lime compounds, silica gels, manganese nodules, gold, ura-
nium. The human being was there, in embryo, at the birth of
Earth, and of ourselves, too embedded in the surround to bear
witness. In Steiner's very mysterious mystery school, one
learned that Earth and human being were twinned cosmic
creations, their fates inseparably intertwined.

Free of all Darwinian dogma and Lyellian uniformitarianism—
musty Victorian thought productions that have somehow sur-
vived into the twenty-first century—these wild, outrageous
pictures will never be countenanced by the cardinals of contemporary paleontology and evolutionary biology. They are offered
here for you to reflect upon, to put into motion as surely as that
ancient living Earth and embryonic man, to see how their story
sits in your bones and sinew and mind sap. For myself, treading
north and east up the granitic Connecticut coastline, regularly
coming face-to-face with the striated bedrock, I now saw these
layers not as having settled out from "ancient seas," but as the
sparkling memory of a viscous Jell-O Earth setting up as solid,
so that mammals and man and their brethren might come along
later to act out their parts.

The story of our shared history with the animal kingdom is written into their spectacularly diversified forms, but in a much deeper and more meaningful way than neo-Darwinian theory offers us. Perhaps the deepest expression of that shared history is that just as our etheric bodies are turned inside out between incarnations, so too were the etheric bodies of our animal cousins, during the ancient time when the Earth's life sphere was resonant with shimmering etheric forces. The starry group of soul beings once transformed tissues, organs, and bodily structures of Earth's diverse creatures, on the human being's way through the long Lemurian—esoteric paleontology's designation for the Earth ages spanning from the Cambrian to Cretaceous—afternoon.

Rudolf Steiner discovered that the most fundamental gesture at the heart of creation was that of turning outsides into insides, and insides into outsides. He found this delightful gesture at all scales of nature, and, most important, *performed* this gesture throughout his own life, bringing to humanity the most extraordinary gifts. Unlike James Dwight Dana, O. C. Marsh—Dana's protégé whose fascination for pterodactyls imprinted itself indelibly on Yale's Peabody Museum of Natural History when it was founded in 1866, the same year Marsh joined Dana on the Yale faculty—and every paleo-picture-painting geologist and paleontologist since, Steiner *did* time-travel, venturing back via the *akasha* to the birth of Earth, and beyond. When he coined that injunction "*The human being must become a vortex*," he did so out of his own extra-ordinary sensory observations, having seen with his own acutely cultivated third eye that the vortex is stamped into the fabric of creation like no other sigil or sign.

As I walked up the trail to the top of West Rock, I felt min-
gling within myself great gratitude to both Rudolf Steiner and
James Dwight Dana, for their both having faithfully exercised
their senses to their finest and furthest limits. Steiner never saw
West Rock or the Connecticut Valley peneplain; Professor
Dana never swam in the Triassic and Cretaceous Jell-O seas
with ichthyosaurs and plesiosaurs, nor watched pterodactyls
plummet into their gaping jaws. But we—Henry and I and you
now too—can place both sets of pictures inside our souls, and
find the balancing point between human sensing and imagination. We also can cultivate the new sensory capacities that are
our birthright, and which were actually laid down as ancient
albuminous substrate in the Earth body long before we ourselves had bodies. What a promise!

By the time I reached Judges Cave at the top of West Rock,
the rain that had been falling all morning had begun to turn to
snow, and I considered taking shelter in a crevice of that
"cave"—more a cracked glacial erratic than broken bedrock
shelter. But I was keen to reach West Rock's south-facing over-
look of Professor Dana's town. There was a plaque on the
boulder that tersely told the story of the outlaw judges: in
May 1661, Edward Whalley and his son-in-law William Goffe,
members of the Parliament General and officers in the Army
of the Commonwealth, had hidden out here while on the
lam from officers of the Crown sent by King Charles I, whom
they had previously judged as guilty of high treason, con-
demning His Highness to death. The plaque carried beneath
this capsule history the unattributed quotation OPPOSITION

TO TYRANTS IS OBEDIENCE TO GOD, with the date 1896. It seemed something that Henry would have said, or any American facing the child tyrant currently occupying the Oval Office.

A short walk and I reached West Rock's precipitous summit, clad in red cedar and shrub oak poking out of the black traprock. Below, Yale's compact colonial-era campus spilled centrifugally across the New Haven plain, a dozen new towers springing up—each one telling which new science was in vogue, and thus awash in dollars. The level horizon, no matter how outdated I knew "peneplain" theory to be, still appeared to my eyes and mind as an eroded plateau, à la William Morris Davis and James Dwight Dana both. Perched atop a ledge, updrafts off the cliff shaking the dry brown oak leaves, I felt like saying a prayer.

"Thank you, James Dwight Dana, for trying to sense your way into Earth history. Thank you, Rudolf Steiner, for turning yourself inside out, and pointing the way for us to do so. May we, in time, take the place of the pterodactyls, and become Earth's eyes."

Just as I finished the prayer and opened my own eyes, I saw a pair of pterodactyls approaching from the peneplain horizon. Enormous black silhouettes against the gray sky, their forms grew clearer as they made straight for West Rock. I could clearly see their great beaked heads, and the scimitar-shaped wings. I squinted to make out the creepy dewclaws at the bend in their wings, as they came directly overhead, then turned and flew off toward the east. It was only after they had become dark pinpoints again against the peneplain horizon that I realized they were great blue herons, metamorphosed by my own imagination.

❧

HENRY THOREAU FAMOUSLY had the most acute senses—of seeing, hearing, smelling, tasting; to each sensory domain, he brought focused powers of attention. As we moderns narrow our senses to accommodate the digital imperium, we have attenuated and atrophied our sense life. The tragedy is that this is occurring at the very moment in Earth and human evolution when we are destined to unfold *new* senses that will enable us in time to turn the Earth inside out, and with that invagination, perform the same magic feat with our own bodies. The rare, unusual clairvoyances of today will become the everyday sense of tomorrow.

We *attend* with our senses. Sharpen yours perennially and perpetually. Notice your noticing: *see* your seeing; *listen* to your listening; *taste* your tasting; *smell* your smelling; *touch* your touching. If you do just this, you will soon and surely find that a sixth sense arises from your five.

#5: SENSE your way toward the extrasensory.

CHAPTER 6

Gone Fishin': SYMPATHIZE!

His hat made of an oaken leaf,
His shirt, a spider's web,
Both light and soft for his fine limbs,
Which were so smally bred.

His hose and doublet thistle down,
Together weav'd full fine,
And stockings of the apple green,
Made out of the outer rind.

His garters were two little hairs,
Plucked from his mother's eye,
His shoes made of a mouse's skin,
And tanned most curiously.

Thus like a valiant gallant he
Did venture forth to go,
With other children in the street,
His pretty pranks to shew.
—THE FAMOUS HISTORY OF TOM THUMB,
WHEREIN IS DECLARED, HIS MARVELOUS ACTS OF
MANHOOD FULL OF WONDERFUL MERRIMENT (1775)

HENRY LOVED STORY, and stories. "To the thinking mind," he declared, "the whole world is enveloped in mystery, and everything is full of type and portent." Thus armed, this hunter of portent pursued the strange and remarkable, passing easily from a youth spent delighting in Mother Goose rhymes and chapbook tales to an adulthood dedicated to the mysteries of nature and history. He loved the stories of the Three Wise Men of Gotham; Jack Horner; Jack the Giant Killer; Robin Hood; Dr. Faustus; Fortunatus; and Tom Thumb. These tales were raw and bawdy, and all their protagonists' triumphs and trials appeared to happen by chance, thus making their biographies seem absolutely fated.

In his unbridled affection for Tom Thumb, Henry was in good company. "Who," asked a seventeenth-century chapbook writer, "but little Tom has made long nights seem short, and heavy toyles easie?" Tom's fame had endured for over two centuries in old England; it would not be until a century after the Revolution that comic characters like the Yellow Kid and Little Nemo would eclipse the wee hero. Tom hovered like gossamer between the real and make-believe as much by his Lilliputian stature as by his Brobdingnagian exploits, and shared with every child who fell in love with him the sense that being small was a blessing, not a curse.

Henry's affinity for wee creatures stayed with him into adulthood. Let other naturalists champion mighty redwoods and colossal elks. Mice and baby turtles and spring peepers were plenty majestic for him. Darwin never lost his love for beetles; Marsh and his fellow dinosaur hunters had, like all children everywhere and always, started out as insect fanciers, bugs being the Tom Thumbs of the animal kingdom.

In New Haven, I had been hosted by my friend Gar Waterman, who was at that moment engaged in a fantastic enterprise of scaling creatures up for an inventive exhibition at Yale's Peabody

Museum. "Beauty and the Beetle: Coleoptera in Art and Science" would pair the museum's unparalleled beetle collection with Gar's gargantuan steel sculptures of coleoptera, fashioned from the mountain of machine parts he had salvaged decades before from a West Rock scrapyard. Scaled up a hundred times from their natural size, Gar's beetles were metallic monsters, their pincers truly— rather than just figuratively—menacing. The beetles' beastliness was accentuated in Gar's studio, where his diminutive *Tin Men* sculptures, tinkered out of the same machine scrap repository, perched on windowsills and shop tables. With solder and steel, Gar had elevated animals over man, consistent with his (and Henry's and mine as well) estimation of human folly.

As I put on my pack to head for Old Saybrook after a short stack of Gar's banana pancakes, he bade me adieu by calling to mind Ratty and Mole's surrender to Toad's gypsy caravan adventure.

"*Wind in the Willows!* It's my birthday, and I ask but one gift—a copy of *Wind in the Willows.*" I had already been granted another wish, for the previous evening, as the *Captain of a Huckleberry Party* gathering drew to a close, a woman in the audience offered me her home for the night after my performance. It was to be a Toad-worthy shelter, it seemed, for she said she would send her driver around to fetch me. Her friend then added that I might come to dinner beforehand. I felt like Mole when Toad unloaded his ample picnic basket on the riverbank, even though I'd not as yet taken a single step toward the Wild Wood of Old Saybrook.

As I stepped through the back door of Acton Public Library in Old Saybrook, I overheard a woman in the hallway say "Thoreau" and "Walden" to another woman. They were standing in the middle of a couple of dozen boxes of books—the library's spring book sale. Dropping my pack in the hall, I asked if there was a children's book section, then made straight for the next room, which was bulging with more boxes. I poked into one, but lazily concluded it might take an hour to go through all the books. I stepped back into the other hallway and asked the woman I had heard pronounce "Thoreau" if she had perhaps noticed a copy of *The Wind in the Willows*.

"Oh, I just saw it a minute ago," she said as she led me back to the children's books. Reaching into a box, she flipped a few titles forward, and pulled out a beautiful 1966 "Junior Deluxe Edition" of Kenneth Grahame's classic—illustrated by Tasha Tudor.

Eureka! Extra-vagant wish granted, I slipped it into my pack, and headed upstairs to the room where I would be speaking. A workshop was just ending; a trio of community organization representatives had led three dozen people in a training on how to support local immigrant communities. As they filed out of the room, one could see their determination and solidarity. I could feel Henry smile, and thought of his question: "How can I understand the rock, unless I can soften toward it?"

When Henry was a boy, every American parent knew the transformative power of *sympathy*, of "softening" toward other creatures, both human and nonhuman. In that industrializing era, woods and fields were still close enough that all but the most urbanized kids could soften toward spiders, beetles, salamanders, crayfish, minnows, and myriad other mysterious but inviting animal beings, and thus practice softening toward fellow human beings. What an easy way to learn unconditional love!

Walking the Connecticut coastline parallel to I-95, I couldn't help but notice that some of America's finest natural history writers called this coastline home—Roger Tory Peterson in Old Lyme; Anne Morrow Lindbergh in Darien; Joseph Wood Krutch in Redding. Here, where one after another sweet river ran down to empty into Long Island Sound, even one named the Thames after that same English river where Grahame's menagerie adventured, were salt marshes and brackish bays, nurseries for endless animals toward which any boy or girl might sympathetically soften.

When Vermont poet Walter Hard in 1947 tried to put the Long River's epic history into one book, he might have celebrated characters like Tom Thumb and Mole and Ratty who populated its banks and mid-channel for a dozen generations. Instead, in the hagiographic tradition of New England historical writing, he picked safe, standard characters and events—Samuel Morey's invention of the steamboat before Robert Fulton; Daniel Webster's Dartmouth oration; Augustus Saint-Gaudens's love of the covered bridge he could see from his Cornish studio; the Estey Organ Company in Brattleboro. A river as long as the Connecticut has a thousand hermits, pirates, peddlers, and misfit fools of lesser fame than Henry Thoreau along its banks, but nary a one ever made it into either Hard's *Rivers of America* title or any other classic descriptions. Perhaps the closest candidate for folklore immortalization was the subject of the poem "The Old Leather Man," a mysterious vagabond who was itinerant through dozens of Connecticut towns in the late nineteenth century. Newspapers followed his circuit for decades, and he was often reported in the riverbank town of Essex. In 1875, for example, Old Leather Man "as usual stopped at the house of Billy Starkey and partook of hot coffee, cake, and pie as he has done for the past 20 years. He makes his trips every six weeks. He is always on time and never fails." In 1886, when he failed to show in mid-February, rumors spread that he had died during the recent cold snap. But then he stopped at another Starkey clan member's house to get his lunch. When, in 1888, he failed to stop at his accustomed place, newspapers reported that he took a different route, on account of following the railroad due to it being free of the deep snow that covered the roads that spring. His route also included East Haven, North Haven, Madison, Guilford, Old Saybrook—exactly the itinerary I was following.

Why did no one know his name or history? Had no one softened toward this leather-clad, peregrinating rock of a man?

Despite being as richly riparian a region as Old England, New England has never fledged a children's tale of love, wisdom, and homespun heroism to rival *The Wind in the Willows*. American children in this third century after American independence are still raised on a diet of Tolkien and J. K. Rowling. The bestselling *American Gods* is by the Brit Neil Gaiman; of course Harry Potter is also from "across the pond." What about our *native* ponds and rivers, which have produced *Walden* and Huck Finn and Tom Sawyer, but no fantasy comparable to *The Wind in the Willows* or *The Lord of the Rings*?

Natural history, the art and science of knowing beings primarily through some process akin to Thoreau's sympathetic softening, is and has been for decades largely a dead letter in America. Most young fingers and hands become intimate with screens and keyboards long before they fondle their first fish or place fireflies inside a mayonnaise jar, net butterflies, or trap beetles. Rock, mineral, seashell, fossil, flower, and other natural history collections are now a scarcity, and with that scarcity a profoundly unsettling "hardening" has replaced the softening called for by Henry.

ℬ

THE DAY BEFORE I sat down to write this chapter, a new friend recommended I go to see *Guardians of the Galaxy Vol. 2*. I have summoned within myself every ounce of goodwill, of tolerance, of softening that I can, and still I am left with a sickening nausea just to recall a single scene from this disgusting depravity. I grow sicker when I think of the eight- and nine-year-old children peering over their popcorn in that Saturday afternoon pornographic riot of violence, mayhem, cynicism, and sadism. I run through the cast of trickster characters from my own childhood—Bugs Bunny, Road Runner, Ignatz, Baron Barracuda from the underwater puppet show *Diver Dan*, even Alfred E. Neuman—and can find no literary precedent for "Rocket Raccoon," the foulmouthed, murderous sidekick in *Guardians of the Galaxy*.

The Tom Thumb, the Mole, of *Guardians of the Galaxy* is called "Groot," as in "Baby Groot," a tiny, wizened, treelike being. Though the Marvel-supplied backstory and character development do not cast him as an orphan like the strutting hero Peter Quill, Groot is certainly orphaned—and foolish, continuously making slapstick errors. His power of "softening" the viewer's heart is magnified by the scale and intensity of violence exploding all around him. Yet Groot himself is a cold-blooded killer, a screaming banshee who can grow roots and branches that become guillotining lassos. In the tenderest of *Guardians of the Galaxy*'s forest scenes, Rocket Raccoon counsels little Groot not to press the red button that will destroy the universe.

Tom Thumb, born into the close village world of Old England, held no delusions of being a "guardian of the galaxy," but proved his mettle enough by surviving: his fall into the Pudding Bowl, and escape out of the Tinker's Budget; being tied to a thistle, then eaten by a grazing cow; swallowed by a Giant after being abducted by a Raven. In *The Wind in the Willows*, when Toad, Mole, Ratty, and Badger do battle with the Weasels, it is all over in an instant. No blood is shed, no heads cut off, no slow-motion CGI sequences of a dozen bodies pierced by Yondu's whistle-controlled assassin's dart. The fearsome four foes of the Weasels in *The Wind in the Willows* do wield wooden cudgels to repulse their enemy, and even utter fierce battle cries—"I'll pleasure 'em!" yells Toad; Groot-like, Mole cries, "A Mole! A Mole!" "What a squealing and squeaking and screeching filled the air!" the narrator mildly summarizes for us.

The vanquishing of the Weasels in *The Wind in the Willows*' final scene—"The Return of Ulysses"—is mere stage setting for the insufferable gasbag Toad to recite in song his own heroics. But, to the surprise of all, after singing "Fool's Last Little Song," Toad gives all the glory to his companions, and declines when asked to give a speech. "He was indeed an altered Toad!" exclaims the narrator.

For all the martial bluster in his intensely chivalric soul, Henry rarely stooped to battle scenes to convey heroic valor and glory. "You may perhaps have some pleasant, thrilling, glorious hours, even in a poorhouse," Henry counsels in the conclusion to *Walden*. *What* in the world, one wonders, is the human heart expressing in this current global explosion of souped-up super-hero spectacle, not just in the Hollywood "franchises," but in the narcissistic riot of X Games and YouTube productions and three-year-olds sporting Wonder Woman and Superman T-shirts? *Where* in the world have Tom Thumb and Mole re-treated to? Have they abandoned the Earth for some quieter planet, where testosterone-driven freaks are not running ram-pant? And *who* in this world will stand up in the middle of the crowded matinee and shout: "Parents! Grab your children and run to the riverbank! Make haste! Meek muskrats and moles, brave badgers and bank swallows, and even spiderweb-shirted Tom Thumb are waiting for you there, keen to connect with you and your children, to soften your soul into warm riparian sympathy with them. Please! Stand up! Now! Go!"

Guardians of the Galaxy opens with the marathon battle of the so-called "Guardians of the Galaxy." What a conceit! As if bratty, self-absorbed bullies would guard anything but their own bloated egos! These consistently anti-heroic heroes wage frenzied war against the titanic pink, warty, tentacled grub. *Walden*'s last lines, unsurprisingly, are a Yankee folktale, of the "strong and beautiful bug" that hatches out of a farmer's vener-able apple-wood kitchen table, having been imprisoned as a tiny egg in the living tree sixty years before.

When Henry said that, in baiting his line when out fishing on Walden Pond, he aimed to catch "two fish on one hook," he di-rected our attention to the subtle spiritual realm above, where each of our thoughts, our impulses, can act either as sweet nectar for benevolent beings, or foul scraps attracting flies—malevolent demons. Henry surely is saying, in those last lines of his great masterpiece, that we ourselves are the bait for miracles, when he asks: "Who knows what beautiful and winged life, whose egg has been buried for ages under many concentric layers of woodenness in the dead life of society . . . may unexpectedly come forth from amidst society's most trivial and handselled furniture, to enjoy its perfect summer life at last!"

Be, dear reader, the bait for miracles, for angels, for your fellow beings. Soften even to the rock! Put Tom Thumb upon your shoulder, and Mole in your pocket in case of emergencies. Study the aerial antics of barn swallows and bank swallows and swifts, so that you too might gambol so gloriously. Turtle and toad too can teach you things about being human, and humbly so.

#6: SYMPATHIZE yourself into the Creation, both large and small, and you shall become the bait for miracles.

CHAPTER 7

Making Worlds: BEFRIEND!

TWENTY YEARS BEFORE I became the Captain of a Huckleberry Party, I had passed through New London in five successive Septembers just after Labor Day, to join my parents and siblings for a reunion out at Montauk, down the beach and a short swim from Hither Hills State Park, where we had camped behind the *Rosa rugosa*-topped dunes every summer since I was eight or nine. Always late for the Orient Point ferry, I would jump off the interstate and dash down State Street to queue up for the ferry. One September I was on time, and stopped to get a sandwich in the Thames River Greenery, a deli and grocery a couple of blocks from the big brick Union Station—a Henry Hobson Richardson creation. Having driven for four and a half hours straight from northern Vermont, I was so grateful to be greeted warmly by a tall, lanky black man who was standing in the entryway.

"Welcome to New London, brother!" the stranger said.

A long solo drive drains one's life force, in a way that a long walk does not, and the man's fraternal hospitality instantly lifted me up. While I ordered a sandwich, he continued to play host with me; as I left, I distinctly recall feeling I had a friend in New London. A year later, boomeranging back for another family reunion, I made a beeline for Thames River Greenery, thinking I might see my hospitable friend. Sure enough, he was standing there on the tiled mosaic floor greeting whatever part of the world happened through his door.

Sequestered in my car, I had never noticed the gorgeous turreted brownstone Public Library of New London building standing at the top of State Street. Approaching it on foot this last Sunday of March, the first thing I saw was a plaque dedicated to the library's patron, whaling magnate Henry Philemon Haven. Another bronze sculpture hovered over the fountain at the library's entrance. Above a pair of leaping whales stood a man holding an open book aloft in his left hand, a woman bearing a whale weathervane in her right. I had no idea that New London had been a whaling town, nor a leader in the West Indian trade.

"Whaling magnate"? Where does such an expression come from, and what does it really signify? In my case, I was merely quoting the interpretive sign on the brownstone portico columns. Downtown New London along State Street and Bank Street is as rich in historic plaques of various generations as it is in gorgeous historic buildings, stretching from before the Revolution up through the tiny town's industrial glory days in the early twentieth century. A prosperous maritime community since its founding by the remarkable John Winthrop the Younger in 1646, the town's rhythms of economic, social, and spiritual development are obscured by the most well-intentioned and -executed markers. One of the first signs I bumped into suggested just how thoughtful the most recent phase (by New London Landmarks) had been: at the foot of Huntington Street, where one could stand and gaze upon four of the grandest of the town's dozens of churches, there was a historical marker that very understatedly gave expression to the perennial factionalism between Christian denominations in New London.

Underneath the heading "Religious Diversity," the wry text read: "New London's first English settlers, Puritans, did not consider religious tolerance a virtue. They would probably be dismayed to see the diversity that now prevails." There were great historic photographs of six churches, all located on a map, with a legend that gave historical and architectural notes. Then, over in the lower left-hand corner, was a gray sidebar titled "Reverend Jabez Swan." It told of the Huntington Street Baptist Church's founding pastor's dislike for the Universalists, whom he warned in 1842, as they were raising up their new church: "Now plan and build a good house. Build no small thing for the Lord. The Baptists shall yet possess the house, and I expect to stand in its pulpit and preach."

Only seven years later, the Universalists were broke, which forced them to sell their fine new building to the Baptists. The gloating Reverend Swan then mounted its pulpit just as he had foretold.

B

A BRONZE BAS-RELIEF always speaks "august," especially when sculpted by Augustus Saint-Gaudens, New England's and perhaps America's most celebrated progressive-era celebrant of the past in stone and metal. Henry P. Haven looks out with love from his brownstone bibliophilic gift upon all who passed by, blessing them with his high brow and bushy sideburns and tightly pursed lips. Like a million other statues, he defaults into type, though the whole intent is to delineate a unique and admirable individual.

Born up the Thames at Norwich, like so many of New London's leading citizens (and darkest rogues—including Benedict Arnold, who ordered New London burned to the ground on September 6, 1781), Henry P. Haven was orphaned from the care of his mother at age four, and moved to New London at age fifteen, where he was indentured to the leading whaling merchant Thomas L. Williams. Eight years later he had become Williams's partner, sending out the city's first steam whaler, which returned after fifteen months with a cargo of whale oil and bone valued at $150,000; Haven, Williams and Company came to control the entire Alaskan seal business. Haven and Williams's ships visited the uttermost parts of the Earth, bringing home cargoes from the coast of Brazil and Patagonia; the icy realms of the Arctic and Antarctic; the islands of Japan; the bleak shores of Kamchatka and Labrador. When whale oil was replaced by petroleum, his firm profited mightily from mining guano on Pacific bird islands.

By turn bank officer, state representative, and mayor of New London (he was defeated as governor in 1873), this large, portly, handsome, affable, and generous citizen of the tiny town was in his own mind merely a faithful servant of the Creator, a devoted Sunday school teacher and innovator, serving for thirty-seven years at Waterford's Gilead Sunday school, then sixteen at the Second Congregational Church of New London. In a sketch of Henry P. Haven as a "model superintendent," Henry Clay Trumbull said Haven had learned well the most important Sunday school lesson—to avail yourself of an instrument fit to your measure, and no further: as a boy he chopped firewood for his mother's household. Being too small to wield an ax, he made a hatchet do double duty.

At age twenty-one, Henry P. Haven had begun his little Sunday school with nine scholars, in Waterford, "a place . . . of vilest repute, and a sink of iniquity by the worst class of evildoers." As did he about the training he received from the teenage Harriet Lathrop, hundreds of his students ascribed their success in life to the regular and rhythmic training they received from Superintendent Haven, who at precisely nine fifteen would tap his bell for attention, then, after a brief wait for perfect silence, read with his pupils the same three texts of Scripture, followed by a chant and a hymn of worship.

What a very long way from Desolation Island such a tender and mild routine seems! And yet, all about the town, it is the whale, not the Sunday school bell or hymnal, that holds pride of place. Down State Street's gentle length the leviathan is commemorated upon shop shingles; a vast two-story-high mural; the city pier; and a graceful fountain at State Street's foot, across from Union Station. Along Bank Street, where once were piled rotting whale carcasses and bleached bones, taverns and cafés offer microbrews and fair-trade coffee in glasses and mugs adorned with the mammoth-headed, tiny-eyed creatures.

It is by no conscious act of deception that such sentimental images saturate the New London streetscape. Simple selective remembering and the deeper tide of forgetting have long ago shaken off any more visceral pictures of this bloody industry. That three generations of New London's boys went off to club baby seals must never have been too happy and proud a claim. Some far-off twenty-first or twenty-second century monuments to the memory of the two riverbanks fledging nuclear submarines—mammoth machine leviathans that eat nations rather than tiny krill or microscopic plankton—will no doubt similarly sanitize memory.

ℬ

How, THEN, do we make a world, our world? It comes to us with our mothers' milk, and with each word and image of our childhood, when our senses are attenuated and alive with participatory, raw zeal. We are at birth the fish's lateral line all over, the seal's whiskers, the whale's sonar. We shimmer with sensation, in a world of sounding, shining sense.

Given primordially and eternally by the gods, our world then in the dim mists of the past (and for every one of us in the present) is mediated, motivated, and metamorphosed by our fellow humans. Mother, father, sister, brother, neighbor, nemesis, strangers, friends all come like waves to beat upon the shores of our souls, engraving lines and curves and circles upon our subtle bodies—a kind of invisible tattoo of the most mysterious and sublime order.

The supposed misanthrope Thoreau was anything but, and he of all the Concord circle offered in his solitary self a singular study in *phil-anthrophy*, not *mis-anthropy*. In an era when romantic and fraternal love were finding new outlets of expression, the hermit of Concord was mapping out his own world not by pushing away from his fellows, but by diving more deeply toward them. Having declared in November 1850 that he would make his journal a record of his love, Henry honed his already acute skill for reading and responding to human gestures. Science by 1850 was entirely analytic, always attempting to reduce complexity and ambiguity by taking living and nonliving things apart. Henry, by contrast, enlarged understanding by seeking wholes and then rendering them synthetically. He belittled naturalists for not being more attentive to color, believing that in both animals and plants, "color expresses *character*." Human gestures fascinated him as well: "Why do laborers," Thoreau asked, "so commonly turn out their feet more than the class still called gentlemen, apparently pushing themselves along by the sides of their feet?"

"Worlding" for Henry very much included *leaving* the world of the senses. Given since boyhood to spontaneous ecstasies, by his late thirties he regularly walked into forest swamps or across riparian sandbars and right out of this world into another. On an "aggravated November" day (called such by Thoreau for the lack of snow on the ground) in December 1855, Henry was

threading his way through a spruce swamp tangle, when suddenly:

> My body is all sentient. As I go here or there, I am tickled by
> this or that I come in contact with, as if I touched the wires of a
> battery. I can generally recall—have fresh in my mind—several
> scratches last received. These I continually recall to mind, re-
> impress, and harp upon. The age of miracles is thus returned . . .
>
> Beauty and music are not mere traits and exceptions. They
> are the rule and character. It is the exception that we see and
> hear. Then I try to discover what it was in the vision that
> charmed and translated me. What if we could daguerreotype
> our thoughts and feelings! for I am surprised and enchanted of-
> ten by some quality which I cannot detect. I have seen an attri-
> bute of another world and condition of things.

In the ecstatic condition, with his etheric body slightly lifted
out of its physical casing, Henry easily felt the electric "breeze"
of the earth's own subtle body, and the effect was to heighten his
sense of the fit physiognomy of nature. At the time, Louis Da-
guerre's new invention was dazzling the world with its capacity
for reproducing nature. Like the daguerreotype subject who had
to sit for long periods of time in order for an image to develop,
Henry had to remain attentive and still for long periods in order
to receive the crystalline, finely etched impressions that were
characteristic of his perception. "It is only necessary to behold
the least fact or phenomenon," he concluded, "however familiar, from a point a hair's breadth aside from our habitual path or
routine, to be overcome, enchanted by its beauty and signifi-

cance." This was the talent of the physiognomist, to heighten meaning by tilting the head slightly, thereby catching the accentuated relief of surfaces too long seen as flat and featureless. This is the way to *make* a world, your world, not just passively accept the given.

Henry was much more given to chronicling and elaborating upon the world outside himself than he was to the careful consideration of his own biography. In 1856, reflecting on the tracks of his own past, he exclaimed: "In a true history or biography, of how little consequence those events of which so much is commonly made!" He found that most of the important events in his life, "if recorded at all," were undated. He also was struck by how difficult it was for most people even to recall in which towns or houses they had lived, and when.

It is not surprising that in the one small place in his journal where he thought back on his own life, Henry's attention was *physiognomic*. He reminisced on Fast Day (April 10) of baseball games played on the snow-free fields near Sleepy Hollow. "I am sometimes affected," he mused, "by the consideration that a man may spend the whole of his life after boyhood in accomplishing a particular design; as if he were put to a special and petty use, without taking time to look and appreciate the phenomenon of his existence." The very morning after he made this heartfelt plea for self-reflection, his uncle Charles died. His mother's brother had forever been the family member whose eccentric gestures—his clownish facial expressions; his falling asleep mid-sentence; his trick of tossing his hat tumbling into the air and then catching it on his head—made the strongest impression on Thoreau.

Gestures are what we fall in love with, the expressions that catch our eye and delight us to the bone. The day of his uncle Charles's burial, Thoreau memorialized him with but one thought—that he had been born in February 1780, the winter of the Great Snow, and that by dying in another winter of much snow, Uncle Charles had a life "bounded by great snows." When he was becoming estranged from his dear friend Waldo, Henry employed gestural language to sound his lament: "I come here to be reminded of the past, to read your inscriptions, the hieroglyphics, the sacred writings." "Love is a thirst that is never slaked," he declared. "Under the coarsest rind, the sweetest meat. If you would read a friend aright, you must be able to read through something thicker and opaquer than horn. If you can read a friend, all languages will be easy to you." Henry's facility for reading physiognomies actually freed him from the constraints and possible pitfalls of language. Ultimately, he relied on pure gesture to know the status of his friendships.

You know about a person who deeply interests you more than you can be told. A look, a gesture, an act that to everybody else is insignificant tells you more about that one than words can. (How language is always found to serve best the highest moods, and expression of the highest truths!) If he wished to conceal something from you it would be apparent. It is as if a bird told you. Something of moment occurs. Your friend designs that it shall be a secret to you. Vain wish! You will know it, and his design. He says consciously nothing about it, yet as he is necessarily affected by it, its effect is visible to you. From this effect you infer the cause.

Have you not already anticipated a thousand possible accidents? Can you be surprised? You unconsciously through sympathy make the right supposition. No other will account for precisely this behavior. You are disingenuous, and yet your knowledge exceeds the woodcraft of the cunningest hunter. It is as if you had a sort of trap, knowing the haunts of your game, what lures attract it, and its track, etc. You have foreseen how it will behave when it is caught, and now you only behold what you anticipated.

"A friend tells all with a look, a tone, a gesture, a presence, a friendliness," thought Thoreau. "He is present when absent."

And so it is also with the *world's* infinite gestures. The *world*—Sun and Moon and stars, but above all the Earth and all that is in and upon it—gestures toward us at every turn! In meeting those gestures with open or closed heart, we make our world, that very world that will accompany us every step of our journey. With breathtaking speed, every single gesture of humanity or Earth goes from wonder, mystery, and marvel, to prosaic, routinized, given. *We* must turn the given upside down and inside out, befriending it by our attention. *We* with our senses and our soul stay the tide of stultification that will drown us but for our own heartfelt activity of will.

Henry's era was one resonant with "sympathetic" sciences and arts, and produced an as yet still unexhausted reservoir of sensitive portraits of the interior self as it moved into modernity. When I walked into New London, and into Henry P. Haven's lovely library, I had no idea that I'd also walked into the hometown of one of Henry's generation's most brilliant, witty, and deeply honest diagnosticians of the New England soul, Frances Manwaring Caulkins. "Fanny" did this through beautifully balancing her observations of others with her own inner worlds. She was a true sister of Henry for her making mythology out of Yankee folktales; for her fierce allegiance to freedom wedded to both justice and self-discipline; and for her proclivity for examining her own limitations and expanding her possibilities.

In Norwich, the director of the library kindly presented me with a copy of Fanny's *History of Norwich, Connecticut*, and I was smitten and stunned by how astute and lively her portraits were. Fanny had left a mountain of manuscript material (initially with her half brother Henry P. Haven, with whom she lived for the last fourteen years of her life) at her death in 1869, and I happily passed an hour down at the Shaw Mansion on Bank Street examining some of her treasures. Opening a big bound alphabetical volume of correspondence, I was greeted by a series of letters to Fanny from Harvard's George Bancroft. The dean of American history was eagerly seeking research assistance from Miss Caulkins. There were dozens of other illustrious correspondents, and the volume included the official certificate of her acceptance into the Massachusetts Historical Society; she was the first woman to be so honored.

The third volume I opened was labeled simply "The Early Life of F. M. Caulkins"—Fannie's manuscript autobiography. She spoke in third person, which only added to the charm, for I had instantly come to think of Frances Manwaring Caulkins as a petite, retiring Victorian woman whose mind was as much on fire as Whitman's, Emerson's, and Thoreau's. The pages before me, even in their objective third person voice, seemed to lift the cover off Fanny Caulkins's tiny skull, to expose her most private experiences. After a tale about a journey with her two sisters when she was a child, she launched into a confession of how her earliest psychic life was totally bound up with the "Boogerman." There were Boogermen in unopened boxes, prohibited places, behind uncommon noises, and at night they lurked *everywhere*. The accomplice both of parents seeking to place limits on their children's behavior and of older siblings' practical joking, the Boogerman terrorized an imaginative child like Fanny, who confessed to being afraid to be alone even in the daytime, and whose "palpitating heart," haunted by this demonic specter, kept her from falling asleep every night of her childhood.

Reflecting upon her demon-haunted childhood, Fanny concluded that "nature makes but few stoics. We are educated to endurance, scourged by the harsh discipline of life into heroism, presence of mind and insensibility." She revealed that the Boogerman was but one of her mind's distempered bugaboos; there were also "undefined throngs of ghosts, Indians, Tories, wolves, serpents, and others." Until she read history for herself, Fanny believed "Regulars" (British soldiers) to be "not more than half-human, possessed of supernatural powers and cannibal propensities." When she came to be a master teacher, Fanny followed the principle of being always "clear and precise" in her instruction, rather than run to fabulation and fancy. Like her half brother Henry P. Haven, and Henry Thoreau, Fanny embraced the idea that an "early intercourse with heaven is the first, second, and third step in education."

𝒷

"THANK HEAVEN, here is not all the world," Henry says at the opening to *Walden*'s last chapter. The cascade of echoes and expansions of that exclamation of relief are so pithy, sensuous, and homespun that the reader is forgiven should he mistake Henry to be speaking of the benefits of extended excursions upon Earth. Each and every aphorism points beyond terra incognita, to the spiritual world:

* "You cannot go to Tierra del Fuego this summer; but you may go to the land of internal fire nonetheless."
* "How long, pray, would a man hunt giraffes, if he could?"
* "Is Franklin the only man who is lost, that his wife should be so earnest to find him?"
* "Explore your own higher latitudes."
* "It is not worth the while to go round the world to count the cats in Zanzibar."
* "Sell your clothes and keep your thoughts. God will see that you do not want society."

At the end of his experiment at Walden, Henry declared he had learned but one thing, which he bequeathed to his reader. If, like him, his reader walked steadily toward the life he imagined, he would "pass an invisible boundary; new universal and more liberal laws will begin to establish themselves around and within him. . . and he will live with the license of a higher order of beings."

Here was Henry's most extra-vagant claim, the one that put him outside the bounds of his neighbors' bourgeois propensities and our own estrangement from Heaven. Henry was not mindlessly mouthing a cliché when he began his inspired *Walden* apotheosis with "Thank Heaven." He was literally, faithfully, gratefully giving voice to his perennial experience, that Heaven was close about him, and so I join my voice to his, exclaiming:

#7: To make your World, BEFRIEND Heaven.

CHAPTER 8

Fires Within and Without: BURN!

"ENTHUSIASM" FOR HENRY always connoted its Latin root—*en theos*, the "god within"—and so it was that he found in every Massachusetts wood and field and stream the gods that had been overlooked by other naturalists. Along with Minerva, Ceres, Nereus, and Triton, Thoreau attended to the lesser gods of nature. In "Natural History of Massachusetts," a classically canny Thoreauvian survey of his home state's flora and fauna, Henry took readers into beaver lodges and muskrat "cabins"; put them aflight with fish hawks and geese; set them swimming amid the "midnight economy of the fishes." Snakes and snapping turtles he painted with brighter colors than any watercolorist could muster. In support of his claim that "Nature is mythical and mystical always, and works with the license and extravagance of genius," Henry surveyed "crystalline botany"— the parallel working of the formative forces in ice crystals and vegetative growth.

Henry's ability to transcend the prosaic taxonomic cata-
logues rested on observations he made during long, leisurely
walks to favorite Concord-area haunts. Without its citizens' perennial habit of walking, Concord would never have fledged
transcendentalism. All the members of the Concord circle were
great walkers. The rhythmic pulse of walking and talking
forged new friendships, deepened old ones, and created a community of the heart verging on the chivalric orders of old. Henry
declared himself and his walking companions "not equestrians
or Chevaliers, not Ritters or riders, but Walkers, a still more
ancient and honorable class I trust." The transcendentalists
were village people, dwelling in that middle New England landscape between its largest city—Boston—and the strictly rural
region beyond the reach of the railroad and telegraph line, at a
"middling" time in American history, between the Revolution
and the catastrophe of the War for the Union. Henry's claim
that he had been born "in the nick of time" was true both as
playful double entendre and as a triangulation of his place
within the unfolding tapestry of American destiny.

Walking, botanizing, and writing about nature were all re-
spectably common village pursuits in the antebellum era,
though pursued by Henry with uncommon zeal and aptitude. It
is altogether reasonable that he comes down to us as a paragon
of ecologically sensitive stewardship. But the steward of nature's mysteries could occasionally make a misstep. At the end
of April 1844, on a rowboat excursion on the Sudbury River
with young Edward Hoar, son of Concord's squire, Thoreau's
native intelligence slipped momentarily when, as he made a fire
in a pine stump to cook fish chowder, the blaze escaped and

ignited three hundred acres of woodland. Years later, when he reflected on the event in his journal, he did so in the most calm, dispassionate voice, giving us a strange and unsettling feeling as we hear this advocate of ecological responsibility seem to shirk for a moment any responsibility for the ravishing blaze he unleashed on the Concord woods. The trick to seeing and hearing through Henry's charade is to know that this is a true refiner's fire of which he speaks; he sets it as a symbol for soul growth, and so we must enter the retort that he prepares for us. Canny as he may be, even Henry missed the stunning symbolic sequence; less than six months after the fire, toward the end of March 1845, Henry borrowed an ax and, with Emerson's permission, began to cut down some tall white pines on Emerson's land bordering Walden Pond. Understated, humble, with a bit of whimsy, still there was something distinctly phoenixlike about Henry's remove to Walden.

The three and a half years leading up to his move to Walden were truly "excursions," in the original Latin sense of deviating from a direct course. They also set his course for the seminal experience of his life; these were like setting kindling for the larger burn to come. But the truly decisive movement Henry made in those years and in the years to come was his characteristic pulse of heart and mind toward "the love that moves the stars." This movement was subtle enough that it often went undetected and unappreciated by Henry's peers, even Emerson. Both Emerson and Fuller were underwhelmed by two essays published in the fall of 1843 in *The United States Magazine and Democratic Review*. "The Landlord" is Henry's tribute to the art of hospitality. The warm welcoming of strangers into one's household was second nature to Henry, whose own childhood home had been run by his mother as a boardinghouse. Throughout his journals, many of the most moving moments are scenes of hospitality given or received. In the America of Henry's youth, it was still common courtesy to offer traveling strangers bed and board for the night, but Henry always treated such hospitality as an uncommon kindness worthy of the highest praise. He concludes his essay "The Landlord" by ranking the tavern higher than the church, since it is the place where prayers take effect. His constant capitalizing of "Landlord" hints that the model landlord is Jesus Christ.

Dwelling beside and within this crystalline chalice, this alchemical retort for the purification of thought and deed that was Walden Pond, it is not surprising that Henry should meet Christ there. As New England and America freed themselves from old Puritan strictures, Henry freed himself into a revivifying yoga of chastity that placed him at Christ's side. His book *Walden* still ignites a refiner's fire within us, for it is a Christ-imbued gospel. Among the many truths he speaks within its pages, Henry said, "By turns our purity inspires and our impurity casts us down." How are *we* to purify ourselves in this time? Do pilgrimage or putting up a simple cabin for woodland contemplation still work as a device for growing one's soul toward God?

The cabin or three I have built were never at far enough remove from my neighbors to answer that part of the question, but pilgrimages aplenty have I conducted, so here perhaps I have some authority. Like so many suburban kids of my generation, my first pilgrimage took the form of an Appalachian Trail walk the summer of my junior year in high school, and then continued with regular backpacking, canoe camping, and other "wilderness" excursions. Before my daughter was born, I made a solo AT walk dedicated to her. In 1985, to commemorate the one hundredth anniversary of the first botanical expedition to Mexico by the Vermont plant collector Cyrus Guernsey Pringle, I botanized in Chihuahua with a friend, staying at the old hotel where Pringle stayed in Chihuahua City, and tramping the desert canyons where he discovered dozens of new species in the 1880s, at a time when Mexico's flora was as yet unknown to the rest of the world. For a dozen years while living in Vermont, I would on the first Sunday in May circumambulate the bounds of my town, in honor of the old tradition of Rogation Sunday, when the selectmen of two adjoining towns would walk the perimeter of their burghs to make sure that the boundaries were fit and proper. None of these pilgrimages had explicitly spiritual aims and aspirations; they were if anything inspired by the American *civic religion* of environmentalism, or "naturalism"—a kind of unspoken assumption that nature is good, and that if one wanders into it, be it desert, forest, or ocean expanse, one will be healed and made whole, and in the process nature too will receive some benefit.

On the first day of May 2000, while living across the Ottauquechee River from Mount Tom—the birthplace of George Perkins Marsh, the author of *Man and Nature; or, Physical Geography as Modified by Human Action* (1864), which is considered to be the fountainhead of the American conservation movement—I made a "Woodstock pilgrimage." During Marsh's lifetime, the local Woodstock tradition was that each year, on the first of May, all of the children of the village walked to the top of Mount Tom. For most of the decades of the nineteenth century, the children's view from the summit was unimpeded by forest, since, except for occasional hemlock-filled ravines and side-hill woodlots too steep to turn into pasture, merino sheep or Jersey cows had closely cropped the local landscape. The common spring ephemeral plants—bloodroot, wild leek, red trillium, trout lily—that today grow in abundance in the Mount Tom woods in early May were rare and special pleasures for them, confined to the remnant forests that had escaped fire, ax, and plow. Passing the jellied egg masses of wood frogs and spotted salamanders suspended on submerged branches in vernal pools in the Mount Tom woods, I wondered whether the children saw such woodland pools 150 years ago.

That first of May I found that the frogs had all hatched out and were free-swimming tadpoles, but the spotted salamander embryos were still round black spheres of dividing cells, the final form as yet a completely unexpressed idea. A milky-white halo of albumen encircled each embryo, and that in turn was encircled by a clear protective outer sphere, which was in turn surrounded by a spherical gelatinous membrane that enveloped the entire egg mass. I reached into each pool to take hold of the egg masses, which were pierced by the thin stems of maple or oak leaves, to move them into a spot of sun. The four concentric rings looked and felt like a solar system in miniature.

The year before, I had had the opportunity to study embryos up close at the Dibner Institute, during a weeklong gathering of biologists, historians, philosophers, and sociologists of the life sciences at the Marine Biological Laboratory in Woods Hole, Massachusetts. The seminar, designed to get scientists and nonscientists to share questions and ideas with each other, had as its focus the great nineteenth century German embryologist, marine biologist, and philosopher/educator Ernst Haeckel. Despite the august assemblage of intellectuals, there was at every Dibner seminar a distinctly humbling aspect, in that all participants engaged in elementary lab and field exercises designed to acquaint scientist and science studier alike with the rudiments of the particular biological practice in question. For the "Why Haeckel?" session, the organizers felt it was critical that we all have a brief refresher course in elementary embryology, and so, after an afternoon lab session doing microscopic examinations of sea urchin eggs, we moved on to extracting and then examining a living chick embryo. At the end of the lab session, in which we had been witness to the awesome beauty of the embryo's pulsing heart and lungs, one after another pair of lab partners took their petri dishes over to a trash barrel and unceremoniously dumped their embryo before heading for the dining hall. Without giving it any conscious thought, really, I found myself holding my plastic petri dish as I walked across campus to the dining hall, and at lunch I placed the embryo next to me at the table. Every few minutes, I would look down to see if the little heart had stopped beating, for I had asked the laboratory instructor how long I could expect it to live. "Oh, another two or three hours at most." I carried the petri dish with me to the afternoon discussion session, where we debated Ernst Haeckel's theory that ontogeny recapitulates phylogeny— that the unfolding embryo traces in miniature the grand evolutionary unfolding of its ancestral line. My heart would leap each time when, just as I had conceded that the embryo had finally expired, I would notice a small and silent surge of blood that was the telltale of this being's life force. Having only placed a few drops of water in the dish to keep it from completely drying out, I took it to bed with me that evening, and was amazed in the morning to find it still alive. Again the petri dish accompanied me to lab and lecture sessions, until finally, more than twenty-eight hours after I had first placed the embryonic disk onto a little doughnut of lab paper so it could go into the petri dish and onto the light microscope table, the embryo expired. I brought it down to a lovely sand beach next to the laboratory, said a prayer, and buried it.

All the while that I had been in an intense mental act of focusing my attention and intentionality on that embryo, the folks around me seemed not to want to see it, to push it away mentally, especially this mystery of how it had come to stay alive. Instead of eliciting intense curiosity and reverence, the anomalous survival of the chick elicited a reaction not unlike the physical act of dumping the petri dishes unceremoniously after the lab—a sort of willful neglect. The seminar participants seemed to have approached the embryo as if it were stone. And yet we all knew in our heart of hearts that the chick embryo was more of the nature of water—a fluid, vital, and yet resistant to all of our scientific probing, wholly mysterious entity.

A year later I was eagerly anticipating the next Dibner Institute seminar, which was to center on the science of ecology. This time we would be haunting the salt marshes and oak woods rather than the laboratory as we sought to know more deeply the historical conditions that led to the founding of this science in the late nineteenth century. In early spring, I was visiting a Woodstock friend at her winter vacation home in Naples, Florida, and she introduced me to a woman she had recently met—a seventy-seven-year-young astrologer and keen historian of Christianity, who excitedly told me about a pilgrimage that she was to make, with a group called the Sophia Foundation. The pilgrimage—entitled "The Dawn of a New Millennium: The Return of Christ and the Emergence of the Divine Feminine"—was to begin at Chartres Cathedral in France and end at Pentecost on the Island of Iona in Scotland's Inner Hebrides. The journey was explicitly timed to coincide not only with the two thousandth return of the heavens to the configuration they were in around the time of the Divine Birth in Bethlehem, but more particularly with the Saturn-Jupiter conjunction. Such astrological auspices meant nothing to me, since I held astrology in ignorant suspicion. Though a travel tour, the pilgrimage was to have a devotional nature, employing eurythmy, sacred dance, choral singing, and prayer to honor and welcome the earthly entrance of Sophia, the Feminine Face of God that had been so deeply forgotten by Western Christianity for well over a thousand years. The pilgrimage was conceived as sacred work that would resurrect and resuscitate Western culture's connection to Sophia.

My new friend, two days after we met, invited me to go as her guest on this pilgrimage, and I was about to accept the invitation when I realized that it would conflict with the upcoming Dibner Institute seminar. Though I had looked forward to the Woods Hole gathering all year, some inner voice told me that I should not pass up the opportunity to learn something entirely new, so I sent my regrets to the Dibner organizers and made arrangements to join the Sophia pilgrims.

When our daily lives seem sometimes to turn to stone because of repetitive habits of thought and action, we instinctively create for ourselves pilgrimages of a sort—watery, wild, serendipitous, and, if they are truly successful, ultimately mysterious adventures that take us places where we have never been before. For me surely there was plenty of mystery in and about the pilgrimage. I traveled with thirty women and only five men, through lands I had never seen, and never really even thought about, preparing an invisible welcoming chalice for a spiritual being of whose existence I had only just become aware, and to whom I frankly found it nearly impossible to pray; singing unfamiliar hymns and making wholly unfamiliar movements with a group of complete strangers, led by an Englishman named Robert Powell, a former mathematician who now spent his entire life in service to awakening humanity to Christ and Sophia, employing "astrosophy"—an esoteric form of astrology—as his principal tool. I felt surrounded by mystery, or at least my own mystification. Each day I experienced odd and inexplicable happenings, amid a daily regimen of being immersed in contemplation and discussion about a grand sweep of cosmic events, in which our little group increasingly seemed to be active participants. After a week studying the awesome sculptural façades of Chartres Cathedral, our group of pilgrims moved on to southwest England, the land of King Arthur. The day after we arrived at Tintagel and checked in to the Camelot Castle Hotel—a spooky, rambling 1920s hotel directly across from what were purported to be the ruins of King Arthur's castle—I pulled Robert aside and asked him: "Is this a sightseeing tour or a Mystery School?" "Oh, yes, Kevin," Robert said with an impish smile, "this is certainly a Mystery School."

Recent generations of English-speaking children will forever have Hogwarts as their impression of a Mystery School, but for us gray-haired pilgrims, the Mystery Schools to which we paid homage were those of the pre-Christian Druids, where the students suffered intense physical and emotional trials under the guidance of sage leaders—wizards like Merlin, whose magic included giving wings to the massive dolerite blocks from Wales's Preseli Hills to bring them to rest at Stonehenge. At Tintagel, I learned that "Arthur" was actually the name of the leader of a Mystery School that long antedated Christianity, and that a number of historical personalities had later taken "Arthur" as their name in tribute to the original Arthur. The Twelve Knights of the Arthurian Round Table were a picture of the twelve signs of the zodiac, and the cosmic powers contained within them, in service of earthly humanity.

By then I had already undergone a variety of odd experiences at the sacred sites we had visited. At the first site, Woodhenge, only two miles from Stonehenge, I had dropped into the tall grass and lay on my back as the rest of the group—spiraling in at the guide's instructions—entered the stone henge there. As I looked up into the sky, it was clear that the clouds above the site were exactly mirroring the movement of the group, spiraling in counterclockwise fashion. A few moments later, I felt as if an invisible hand had reached into my body and rearranged my bones, followed by a tremendous shaking across my chest.

Frightened, I intuitively moved my arms in the air above my head in the gestures I had been learning in eurythmy, and I could clearly see my arms and hands glowing through my closed eyelids. When I arose I was surging with energy, such that I could literally feel it leaping off of my fingertips and from my chest and forehead. A few days later, at the ruins of Glastonbury Abbey, I walked around barefoot in the cool weather, and found that whenever I stopped walking, I could raise the temperature of the ground below me merely by imagining that I was sending my internal energy down into the ground. On Iona these experiences continued, and still I had no idea why they were occurring or what they meant.

I was as unable to understand these experiences as I had been to understand the survival of the chick embryo. Had I returned to tell my Woods Hole colleagues about them, they would likely have received the news with the same uneasiness that greeted the minor miracle of the chick embryo's survival. The "stoniness" of the human hearts that tossed away chick embryos is representative of a more widespread "turning into stone" among humanity—our belief that the world is essentially a physical creation, governed by physical laws alone. Even at such a magnificent center for the study of life as the Marine Biological Laboratory, where daily the teeming embryonic life of the sea is put into holding tanks, the biologists become workers in stone, since they approach their subject organisms as mere material creations. Indeed, the very vocation—biology—that should most poignantly remind us of our watery nature has more often than not given us an image of living things as mere stone. Ernst Haeckel, a man whose exquisite drawings of the "wateriest" of creatures—jellyfish—would suggest that he valued water over stone, stated in 1877: "The cell consists of matter . . . composed chiefly of carbon with an admixture of hydrogen, nitrogen, and sulphur. These component parts, properly united, produce the soul and body of the animated world, and suitably nourished become man. With this single argument the mystery of the universe is explained, the Deity annulled and a new era of infinite knowledge ushered in." Haeckel's evolutionary reductionism gave philosophical support to the hardening, the petrifaction, of human thoughts about the nature of life.

When Haeckel's contemporary George Perkins Marsh wrote *Man and Nature*, he attended to the *visible*, physical changes that human actions had wrought upon the planet. These changes were there for all to see with their own eyes. The Ottauquechee after every rain ran brown with topsoil washed from the denuded hills, and red or green sometimes after the local woolen mill released dyes. Marsh's book began with the inner pain that he felt upon seeing the Earth ravaged so.

Twenty years ago, Mount Tom became the centerpiece of the Marsh-Billings-Rockefeller National Historical Park, the first national park in America devoted to reflecting upon the history of our relationship with the Earth as stewards of the land and waters. Today, though Woodstock's schoolchildren no longer make the annual May 1 pilgrimage, visitors from all over the world make their own pilgrimage to the summit of Mount Tom, so that it is in the process of becoming a national shrine to conservation, to the sacredness of the Earth in human life. "Sacred" and "secret" share the same root, but it seems that if we are to experience the Earth as sacred, we cannot allow to remain secret those places and events that challenge our beliefs as to what we watery beings are doing on this water planet of ours. When we stand on Mount Tom and any other place today, we need to go beyond *physical* geography to the invisible geography that truly constitutes these places. Just as an invisible umbilical cord was somehow created between me and that pulsing chick embryo, there are gossamer cords running throughout nature and history. This was the main quest of Henry at Walden Pond, and in all of his walking about the Concord hinterland.

Never invited to join a Mystery School, Henry created his own, and then sustained it by solitude and prayer. He especially loved the solitude he found at night, which made it "less profane than day." He preferred moonlit nights not only for the relative ease of travel, but because he could feel Diana's influence upon him then. "Moonshine"—his age's dismissive term for false notions—Henry defined instead as meaning that which men do not understand, or are "abed and asleep to," as they were to the moon. July—when night presented such a cool contrast to day— was his favorite month for moonlit walks: in that month he found whip-poor-wills in place of wood thrushes; fireflies for butterflies; crickets and frogs for singing birds. Shadows became more conspicuous than the objects that cast them, and he could detect variation in topography and vegetation where by day he found sameness. The dark senses—smell, touch, and hearing—took the lead at night, so that he smelled the swamp-pink in the meadow, felt subtle shifts in air temperature, and heard the tinkling of rills he had never detected before. The man who famously declared in *Walden* that "corn grows in the night" could do so because he had smelled, felt, and heard it doing so.

The affinity felt by Henry—who was born just a few days past the new moon—for moonlight was more than just an idiosyncratic response to the opportunities it afforded for altering perception. The full moon had for all of human history been the setting for wild and weird human behavior because lunacy was a physiological fact. The same magnetism that drew high tides higher, propelled potatoes and peas to grow taller, and launched geese and warblers on migration, worked upon the subtle inner oceans of human beings. Witches and wizards—and esoteric orders of the nineteenth century—knew that, as well as moving the physical waters upon the planet, whether held in oceanic reservoirs or the aqueous cells of plants and animals, the moon moved man's subtle organism. At the full moon, the human subtle body was more active, and Thoreau's moonlit rambles always reflected this invisible activity. Diana, charging the atmosphere with "dewy fragrance," gave him "Endymion sleep," an ambrosial sense of having his "dreams awake." The ecstasies he described from his nighttime walks frequently continued into the daylight hours at the period of the full moon, a consequence of his subtle organism being "lifted" slightly out of his physical body, opening him more fully to spiritual currents.

Reading one fall the memoirs of Benvenuto Cellini, Henry was struck by the story Cellini told of a prophetic dream that he'd had one night while confined in the Castel Sant'Angelo in Rome. After this dream, he found that a "resplendent light" appeared over the shadow of his head both morning and evening, wherever he went. Cellini found that it was particularly conspicuous when the grass was moist with dew, something that Henry had observed about his own shadow on certain mornings, and also by moonlight. On one occasion, Henry's nimbus had merged with a rainbow's arch, "dazzling" him: "If it had lasted longer it might have tinged my employments and life." Another time, catching a glimpse of his halo while walking along the railroad causeway, he "fancied [himself] one of the elect." Though he seemed at one level to accept physical science's explanation of the halo around the head's shadow as a simple diffraction phenomenon, he also suggested slyly that there was something more to it. Cellini had shown his halo or "glory" to only a chosen few, and Thoreau pointed out how rarely it was noticed by anyone. "Are they not indeed distinguished," he asked, "who are conscious that they are regarded at all?" The suggestion of divine favor hinted at by the halo was in some of these instances just that, for Cellini's constant aureole and Thoreau's moonlit nimbus occurred when their subtle bodies had been stirred by the moon's forces. The head and hands have always and everywhere been the places where the invisible etheric shroud could most readily be detected; along with discovering his halo, in the same year Thoreau, one full moon day, noticed the "web" running between his fingers: "When I hold mine up to the light & bring them near together— such are the laws of light that just before they touch—a web appears to grow on them & unite them." Unaware that he was viewing his own etheric body—what today is known as the "aura"—he drew from this apparition the lesson that "each thing is attracted to each—& running to coalesce. Like drops of water." In a sense, Thoreau was seeing the medium of magnetism, the vital current that binds bodies—both earthly and celestial—together.

What we do with the mysteries that befall us is the key to our world-making. So-called "paranormal" experiences—twentieth century materialist science's euphemism for "mysteries"—are like gossamer threads that, if not swept aside, will lead us individually and collectively to a renewed discovery of our true human nature, one that acknowledges our immortality as souls. They mark the limits of our contemporary knowledge, where the smug certainty of science must admit ignorance.

℘

OUR SOPHIA PILGRIMAGE itinerary had mentioned that "it may be too early for Crop Circles. However, if there are any to see locally, we shall certainly visit them." I had heard about crop circles for years, and may even have seen a few pictures of them, but all the loose talk about UFOs and spaceships made them completely uninteresting to me. On the way to Avebury, our guide asked our bus driver to pull over at a spectacular bend in the road that offered a sweeping prospect of the Vale of Pewsey, widely regarded by crop circle enthusiasts (it somehow seemed impossible to call the folks who studied them "researchers" or "scientists") as perhaps the most prolific place for their creation. We all moved to one side of the bus and strained our eyes to discern among the waving fields of corn and barley some sign of disturbance. The guide lamented the slow start to that year's crop circle season, and apologized that there was nothing to show us, and the driver eased the bus back onto the road. We had all just gotten to our seats when someone sang out, "LOOK!" Off in the same direction, in a nearby field, the tractor "track lines" led straight out to a large area of flattened barley. We followed the tractor lines out to the circle.

I lay down among the bent plants and pulled one toward me. It was completely normal, except at the node, where the stem made a sharp angle. Each and every one of the "fallen" plants had this same angle in the node, while all around them grew countless normal, erect stems. I had also lain down in plenty of places where deer had also lain during the night in Vermont meadows, and this was nothing like that. It was as if some giant had focused his breath very precisely and blown down a select swath of plants, without killing them or even breaking them slightly.

Back in the bus, as we arrived at Avebury, a huge henge stone circle built around 2650 BC and encompassing about twenty-eight acres, it looked as if everyone in Wiltshire had decided to picnic at the stone circle rather than go to the beach. Though most folks just ambled about, reading the historic signs describing different parts of the site, there were some who obviously were trying to encompass the whole henge, striding purposefully along the outside. Here at least was some visible vestige of Rogation Day. Our crew had their own approach to the site: Fort, a Little John–sized fellow from California, took out his pendulum and started dowsing. A few of the women approached the largest stones, held out their arms, and slowly embraced each stone, with eyes closed, listening for what the stone might say. A couple of teenage boys who were playing cricket while their girlfriends looked on were beside themselves watching one member of our group as she communed with an enormous monolith. They put down the cricket bat and ball for a moment and started tossing playful remarks at her, until she opened her eyes and talked to them. They were convinced that she was deluded, that the stones were just stones, and that crop circles were all made by pranksters.

Directly across the hillside we could see Silbury Hill, a pyramid-shaped mound built around 2750 BC. Known in ancient times as the "Hill of the Shining Beings," it was once an important site for women to perform sacred rituals to the Earth Goddess, and so we gathered at its base to enact our own. Robert intended to lead the group in eurythmy while reciting the "Our Mother" prayer. I was seized with a desire to witness the ritual from the summit of the hill, and asked if I might run to the top to do so. They agreed that one ceremonial celebrant above would be useful, so I began to climb over the barbed-wire fence erected by the National Trust of Great Britain to keep out trespassers. Another member of the group came after me, and when we reached the summit, there was a perfectly round, eight-foot-wide, forty-foot-deep excavation in the very center of the hill. It looked like a giant plug cutter had extracted the core of the pyramid, leaving a neat round ring where the green grass suddenly stopped, and one looked instead at a cross-section of the man-made mound. I had looked down into many holes in the earth in my life, but I had never seen anything like this. Though it was hard to see the bottom clearly, there seemed to be no rubble at the bottom. There certainly was no pile of excavated earth at the top, and I was completely mystified as to where the missing earth had gone. We reported what we had found, but both our guide and a member of our group who had been to the top years ago said there was no such hole in the hill. On the drive back to our hotel, we kept insisting that there was an enormous hole up there, but everyone laughed it off as an exaggeration from the group's most histrionic members.

In every single New England town through which I passed, if I had looked through copies of the local newspaper from the nineteenth century, I would have discovered a whole universe of anomalous events: rains of frogs from the sky; meteors; ball lightning; ghosts; albino deer; two-headed snakes and calves. In the nineteenth century, these were collectively known as "wonders," or, in more modern parlance, "anomalous events." Crop circles are the most conspicuous contemporary example of a "wonder," and they have exactly the same effect upon us as the nineteenth century wonders did on practical Yankees. They tell us that our consensus view of reality needs a bit of tinkering with, if it is to sufficiently accommodate the vast array of phenomena of the physical world.

The Old Testament tells many a tale of this sort of tinkering. In Genesis, in the fire at Noah's altar, the first covenant with Abraham, and the sacrifice of Isaac, Jehovah's flaming sword cut right through the Israelites' perceptual world. Moses in Exodus was forever coming face-to-face with burning bushes and other spectacular signs that there was more to Heaven and Earth than even he dreamt of. In both the Old and New Testaments, these episodes of epistemological correction feature fire as the agent of communication. They are universally *empyrean* episodes, this ancient Greek word retaining the wisdom that whenever Heaven and Earth met, the element of fire (*pyr* = fire) was present. Christ "came to cast fire upon the earth," saying that he was "guarding it until it was ablaze." Though we lit no fires at Woodhenge, Stonehenge, or Silbury Hill, there had been fire aplenty burning in each of these places. And there seemed to be fire burning in the crop circles, even when the clay was saturated with water and dew still dropped off the barley leaves. Looking at the altered node of crop circle plants, one could imagine some sort of "fire" touching the plants just enough to bend them over, then vanishing before setting the plants fully ablaze. Ever since I'd lain down in the grass at Woodhenge, the circling fire inside my chest that threw off rays from my fingertips and feet had grown warmer.

I remember studying the difference between heat and temperature in eighth-grade chemistry class. Mrs. Corrizzi had heated up a pot of water on a burner in the front of the classroom, and after it was boiling she sucked up a little in an eyedropper. Then she stepped from behind the lab table and asked for a volunteer to put his arm out. I jumped up, and she came over and squeezed the boiled water out onto the middle of my bare forearm. "The temperature of that water is nearly 212 degrees Fahrenheit; how hot does it feel?" It felt tepid at best. Mrs. Corrizzi retrieved the pot and came back and held it over my arm. "This water is all the same temperature as the water I just squeezed on Kevin's arm. Will it feel the same to him if I dump the pot on his arm?" There was no need to demonstrate, for we all intuitively grasped that while temperature was the *average* measure of heat in a mass of solid, liquid, or gas, *heat* was the total caloric value of that same mass, and given the volume of water in the pot, I would have received a much larger total dose of heat than had been delivered by the eyedropper.

Eighth-grade chemistry was where I first learned the word "empirical." I remember feeling that it was such a comforting word, that by performing a set of carefully prescribed measurements we could even as fourteen-year-olds compass some significant descriptive truths about the physical world. Both in chemistry and physics, the experiments were set up in such a way that when you came to the end of them, and found that the numbers in your lab book jibed with the numbers in your lab partner's (or some other person's) notebook, there was an immense sense of satisfaction, of completeness, wholeness. Particularly gratifying was the knowledge that liquid water would always turn to ice at 32 degrees Fahrenheit, and to gas at 212 degrees. Having learned the distinction between heat and temperature, we followed the phase changes with great interest, where, despite the addition of heat, there was a slight lag before the new phase was reached.

I cannot recall if it ever occurred to me to question why it was that a certain amount of heat "disappeared" at the times of transition from one state to another. Certainly modern science has agreed not to question it, satisfied with its explanation that the heat that disappears is used in converting matter from one state to another. Not only middling chemistry and physics students fail to challenge this assumption. It is a universally shared blinder, one that in turn shares something with the blinders we tend to don when thinking about "wonders." Given its reliance upon observation and experiment, empiricism relies upon the evidence of the senses, and imparts imperial authority to seeing, hearing, touching, tasting, and smelling. But the simple empyrean phenomenon of phase change is as dramatic as Moses's burning bush for showing how tyrannically imperial empiricism is in its reign.

One physicist who was discomfited by the mystery of the vanishing heat within the change of phase—William Crookes—posited that there was a fourth dimension of space where this missing heat might be found. Crookes is best known for having contemplated another phase change—human life after death—in his fascination with spiritualism, and the history of empirical science has caricatured him because of this coincidence of curiosity. Einstein and relativity theorists felt that if one went outside three-dimensional space, then one entered time, and that it was in time that one accounted for the missing energy. This is an uncanny echo of the solutions posed for the mystery of crop circles. Some "croppies" claim that the "circlemakers" exist in space, outer space to be exact, and are sure that alien beings from other planets—conveniently known now by their acronym LGM, for "Little Green Men"—are responsible for the exquisite formations in the fields. Another camp seeks the solution in time: they interpret these signs of the times as coming from out of the future, a sort of rippling back into the present of human knowledge and technology as it will be centuries or millennia from now. They see the crop circles as reflections of an advanced understanding of nature, where human intelligence can manipulate the natural world with the finesse of the artist.

And then there is consensus reality, the agreed-upon sleep of science and the sleeping giant of mass culture, where the only plausible explanation is that "hoaxers," vandalous artists and mischievous epistemological tricksters, have organized themselves like elves to appear in the night and, with boards and string and a good old college try, flatten the fields for fun. This assumes that one is even thinking about crop circles at all, which 99.9 percent of humanity is not, even if the circles are the most dramatic and potentially communicative mystery on the entire planet.

In the East Field and other locations, the mysterious flattened crops usually took the shape of circular forms. As "data," the descriptive terms used by the researchers for the various circular patterns—"grapeshot," "rings," "dumbbells"—are rather lame, and highlight our inability to wrap our minds around the phenomenon. Very near our circle spot, part of a "face" appeared in July 1994—the "Eye of Horus." The Egyptian sun god Horus was represented always with the head of a hawk or falcon, the right eye as the sun, the left as the moon. The crop circle followed the traditional symbol in its stylized "eyebrow," which looks somewhat like a mathematical symbol. Indeed, after 1200 BC the "Eye of Horus" was used by Egyptians to represent fractions.

Ancient Egypt's fascination with numbers manifested in another East Field crop circle; on the summer solstice of 2001, a perfect pyramid, crowned with a raying Eye of Horus, appeared as the first circle of the season. Perhaps the crop circles were telling the world that one needed the wisdom of ancient Egypt to penetrate their mystery, for the Great Pyramid at Giza was, during the reign of the pharaohs, a desert Chartres Cathedral, a building that single-handedly contained all of the esoteric knowledge of its time, and presented it in a picture language.

Pi, expressed mathematically as 3.1416 . . . , can be derived from the equilateral triangles making up the pyramid, while the golden mean, the most divine building block, *phi*, is contained in the Great Pyramid in the form of its faces, whose slope height (height apparent to the observer) is equal to 1.618 times half its base. The pyramid's vertical height is thus the square root of 1.618 times half its base. When these proportions are translated into the physical realm, they become descriptive of all examples of geometric progression—in other words, of biological growth. From simple cell division to the unfurling palm frond, spiraling leaf nodes around a stem, to the helices of ram horns and hurricanes, and finally to the vortex of galaxies, *phi* and *pi* conspire to make worlds that perpetually circle back upon themselves in a fabulous fractal explosion of form. The giant snail, scorpion, snowflakes, and DNA strands that have appeared as crop circles in the East Field all point in the direction of *phi*. Pointing to *phi*, these figures point to Fire. In the *Timaeus* Plato declares:

> And we must not forget that the original figure of fire (that is, the pyramid), more than any other form, has a dividing power which cuts our bodies into small pieces, and thus naturally produces that affection which we call heat; and hence the origin of the name [fire, or *phi*].

Plato identifies here the "dividing power" of fire, but as the "fairest bond" among the fair in God's tool kit, *phi*/fire/pyramid was also the supreme unifier, able to reach across Creation, even from the spiritual world into the physical. No less than Moses's burning bush, the crop circles, touched by fire, are an expression of where Heaven and Earth meet. Both builder and destroyer, fire no doubt was capable of instantaneously vaporizing hundreds of tons of chalky, clayey Silbury Hill soil, as surely as it could in a split second turn hundreds of thousands of plant stems sideways, in a not-so-subtle attempt to communicate with a chosen but lost people.

ℬ

THOUGH IN WALKING FROM New London to Norwich I was passing through America's most alchemical territory—in the sense that nearly four hundred years ago John Winthrop the Younger planted profound Christian Hermetic seeds there, and employed alchemical techniques both in his healing work and in his governance of the fledgling Connecticut colony—none of this inquiry into the mysteries of Creation was in my meditations. The weather was awful—cold and rainy day after day—and I felt each morning like abandoning the entire enterprise.

Today, in fact, I had on my mind the incubation of a new book, a book about "book magic." All of my life, I had found that books—the physical objects themselves, not the imaginative adventures inside them—were magically charged vehicles for spiritual beings to communicate with human readers. Just the recent experience of having "conjured" *Wind in the Willows* at Old Saybrook, after Gar's invocation of it in New Haven, put my mind running in this direction. I was walking from book sanctuary to book sanctuary, the public libraries that, though now increasingly serving their communities through online digital activity, still were the repository for all manner of collective wisdom and experience *in books*. Beginning in Old Saybrook, when I met librarians I would put to them the question: "What stories of book magic have you heard, or witnessed, or prompted?" To illustrate my meaning, I'd tell the story of Mark Twain's boyhood encounter with Joan of Arc's story through the tumbling page on the Hannibal street, or of how Robert Powell, the first day of our arrival in England, had walked into a tea shop and a book fell into his hands, open at the place of Seamus Heaney's poem "St. Kevin and the Blackbird." Robert had had this sort of thing happen often enough that he bought the book, gave the book to me, and then invited me to read the poem aloud to our fellow pilgrims. That act sealed my destiny as surely as the tumbling page sealed the fate of the young Sam Clemens, or Emerson's question about keeping a journal sealed Henry's.

I had on one occasion in my global history course performed a flying bit of book magic, as I lectured about Marco Polo. We were reading his *Travels*, and I knew that my students, in reading the section where the young Venetian described the Mongol magicians floating cups of wine across the room, needed some dramatic demonstration to prove to them that Marco Polo was faithfully describing what he had seen. Holding up a copy of the *Travels*, I spoke about how, in ancient Rome, philosophers had performed the *Sortes Virgilantes*—using a book of Virgil's poetry as a divining tool. Boldly declaring that one could use *any* book as an *I Ching*, I turned toward the corner of the classroom next to the entrance door and flung the *Travels* into the air. It landed facedown, open, on an overhead projector parked there.

Striding confidently over to it, I lifted the book, waved my finger in the air, and then, letting my finger land on the upper right-hand page, said that whatever passage I read would directly address the very theme that we were now holding in our consciousness.

> Spirits of the desert are said at times to fill the air with the sounds of all kinds of musical instruments, and also of drums and the clash of arms.

It seemed to me that "book magic" would now be in retreat, given the increasing use of e-books and the widespread practice of reading online—both via computer and smartphone. But I also was sure that the elemental beings who could flip open flying books to just the right page for the hopeful diviner could adapt handily to the new technology. As a mill town, Norwich was a place full of wizards and tinkerers, people who had intense—and frequently magical—relationships with the tools of their various trades. As I walked I imagined a Thames River tavern conversation between a whaler or miller or tailor, in which each confessed that elves had on occasion gotten hold of one or another tool of their trade. A little verse presented itself:

A harpooner has his harpoon.
A chef his best knife and favorite pan.
A writer his choice pen will always have to hand.

Clearly, every tool has the potential to become enchanted, charmed. This town that I was approaching, and every other

New England town, must have folklore about some enchanted
object. Could it be that in Norwich's past there had been a moment when the entire community's life had been given a new
direction by a single object, in the way that Mark Twain's life of
writing was born in the instant of finding that page, or Henry's
had been when Waldo asked him if he kept a journal?

Arriving at Otis Library wet and cold and tired an hour
before my program was to begin, I went straight for the local
history room, and opened Fanny's *History*. Fanny's webs in
Norwich were wide and deep and dense. Though she was born
in New London (in 1795), her father's death at sea before she
was born meant that she lived the first twelve years of her life
with her mother and sister in the household of her paternal
grandfather, Robert Manwaring—first on Manwaring Hill in
New London, then in Montville, and, after 1800, in Norwich,
where he ran a general store. What little formal education the
bright-eyed Fanny received was in Norwich. The tale she told
in her manuscript autobiography of besting the older scholars
in the spelling bee was just the tip of the child prodigy iceberg:
at age eight she would write down from memory the lectures she
had heard by Reverend Joshua Williams; by age eleven she had
read the *Iliad* and the *Odyssey* in English translation, and had
begun to tackle Latin; at age twelve, she had read most of the
notable English authors of the seventeenth and eighteenth centuries. Her family members recognized her destiny early, seeing
in her constant scribbling and reading and collecting of tales and
artifacts a harbinger of her becoming the historian of her beloved
Norwich. "What a pity," Fanny wrote late in life to a Norwich
friend, "we cannot colonize the green plains of Norwich with

just the beings we wish and remove there and be 25 years old forever."

When, in 1845, Fanny published her *History of Norwich*, she made it "as complete a town history as the materials would permit," but she stressed that it would not be a mere litany of genealogies, as was so characteristic of all of New England's other town histories published in the antebellum era. In aiming to "avoid profuse laudation," but give "praise where it was due," Fanny fashioned a unique testament to Norwich's past, shot through with Thoreauvian descriptive detail of the landscape, and equally observant appreciation for the intricate, knotty tangle that was every single individual's biography. When she untangled the legend of Norwich's most ill-celebrated son, Benedict Arnold, Fanny seemed to be establishing principles for the reckoning of any life.

Chapter 33 in *History of Norwich, Connecticut* is titled simply "Arnold, the Traitor." How, then, did he become so? Fanny made sure to establish that both his parents were "honest, reputable citizens," even quoting one of her local reliable sources as saying that "Benedict Arnold's mother was a saint on earth, and is now a saint in heaven." How the son of such a mother as this could have become a "proud, obstinate, and unprincipled man" whose character was "spotted with violence, corruption, and treason" was a deep mystery, beyond the ken even of the perspicacious Fanny. Ever alert to and intrigued by the "supernatural," Fanny detailed the seeming curse—of insanity, fire, and hauntings—that for generations lay upon the house where the traitor had been born. She diligently and judiciously separated out fact from likely fiction regarding the details of the burning of New London on September 6, 1781, and very tellingly gave an emblem for understanding the traitor. While clearing him of the darkest deeds ascribed by local legend—Fanny was sure that "the sum of his misdeeds [were] needlessly enlarged"—she reproduced in her book the simple sign from Arnold's New Haven store, which bore as its last line the Latin motto *Sibi Totique*, which she translated to mean "Wholly for himself."

⁂

BY OUR EVERY DEED, our every thought, our every impulse of feeling, thinking, and willing, we *charm*. We are from head to toe our own most spectacular, supercharged magical talisman, radiating darkness or light, despair or joy, hatred or love. By the time we reach our twenty-first year, we have engraved into ourselves, as surely as into white whalebone, a scrimshaw of seven deadly sins or heavenly virtues. Study the lives of colonial- and Revolutionary-era New England's great spirits—the Winthrops, Mayhews, Eliots, Mathers, Watermans, Manwarings, Caulkins, and such—and you will find a treasure chest of human traits as rich as anywhere and anytime on Earth. In a hundred histories like Fanny's Norwich history, one encounters ample material fit for mythologization, of a quality that could ring down the ages as surely as the *Kalevala* or the *Iliad*. The traitor's tale and the healer's—John Winthrop's—tale belong there equally, illuminating for us our own struggles between good and evil, divinity and debauchery.

Henry was a *charmer*; that is, he *charmed* a wide wake of his neighbors then—and us now—by virtue of his purity, his levity, his fidelity. And yet, he was never as much charmer as *charmed*, in his infinite receptivity to those lavish gifts that the world freely offered. John Winthrop was a charmer. Benedict Arnold was a charmer. Even Fanny Caulkins was a charmer. But any faithful study of their biographies will show that we are not here to charm, but to be charmed.

Ceaselessly, dear reader, seek to be charmed by God's magically charged Creation, for if you do, you shall reap rewards of immeasurable value. Lay up your gifted treasures in Heaven, where Henry lay his, and smile to see their inevitable, irrepressible increase, not just now, but in lifetimes yet to come. Without laying any kindling, without ever lighting a match, you shall burn up immense quantities of dross, of poison, of slothful stores of evil that have slipped into your life while you were not watching or listening. There, friends, is *Walden*'s primary teaching, the yoga of purity, and of purification.

#8: Let the Fires within and without BURN away the inessential.

CHAPTER 9

In the Quiet Corner: BREATHE!

I N APRIL 1846, meditating on what the essential nature of the birds, the pines, the pond might be, Henry confessed into his journal his own essential nature: "I silently smile at my incessant good fortune . . . The elements are working their will with me." He had been pondering the not-so-fortunate fates of vanished neighbors at Walden Pond. The pent road just a few paces from his cabin door was one of the few visible signs of a whole community who once made their home where he now made his. That spring he was poking about both in conversation with elder Concordians and along the abandoned road for stories of these "former inhabitants." He tasted the wild fruit from the derelict orchard of ex-slave Brister Freeman, whose wife Fenda told fortunes. In an oak copse near his cabin, he found bricks from the chimney of Zilpha, a black conjure woman whose home and pets English soldiers set afire during the War of 1812. Just across from his bean field was the cellar hole, now filled with sumac and goldenrod, of yet another ex-slave, Cato Ingraham. Henry also learned of Wyman the potter, whose kinship with him across the ages was founded in their both being squatters of a sort.

Not a single long-settled town in America or even the newly settled places of the American West lacked this liminal geographic zone, where the poor and the outcast found homes at society's edge. Henry's tenancy at Walden Woods represented a third generation of marginality on the pond's shores, a self-conscious re-inhabitation of a rejected place, by a social outcast who felt at home anywhere, but at Walden more than anywhere. Coming upon Hugh Quoil's tenantless house before townsmen anxious about its reputation as "an unlucky castle" destroyed it, Henry was affected by the sight of Quoil's old clothes curled up on his plank bed, his broken pipe on the hearth, scattered playing cards on the floor. No sentimentalist, Henry looked upon the bramble- and sumac-filled cellar holes of Hugh Quoil and the other former inhabitants of the marginal lands flanking Walden Pond as mysterious lessons regarding destiny. He neither condemned nor lauded the lives led there, but was bound to them by their very humanity.

Henry's empathic accomplishment in that short *Walden* chapter is all the more remarkable if one considers it alongside Fanny's two Connecticut town histories. As astute and honest and empathic a chronicler as Fanny was, she failed to bring much of a picture of the liminal communities that dwelled generation after generation on the margins of prosperous New London and Norwich. The darkest blot on the paired towns' character, the traitor Arnold, took on his spectral aspect against the backdrop of a titanic, even world-historical event—the American Revolution. Hugh Quoil and company—and their counterparts in the Thames River towns or anywhere else along my route—were silent footnotes to history. These characters neither claimed nor were given by Fanny or a single other New England town historian any voice or visibility.

Henry's capacity for empathy had moved him since 1839 to refuse to pay his poll tax, which he viewed as supportive of a government that permitted slavery. The moral imperative for tax resistance had heightened in May 1846 when the United States declared war on Mexico. In July, on his way into Concord to see the cobbler, he had met up with Sam Staples, Concord's constable and overseer of local tax collection. Asked by Staples to pay his delinquent tax, Henry refused, and was escorted to the town jail. Without informing him, someone (most likely his aunt Maria) paid the tax and he was told in the morning that he was free to go. In a second act of civil disobedience, Henry refused to leave his cell, and Staples ended up throwing him out. His small act went largely unnoticed at the moment, but the hours spent behind bars became the seed experience for a lecture and essay—"Civil Disobedience"—years later that would reverberate through the centuries.

Henry's friend George Melvin, Concord's veteran fur trapper, once told him a tale of a muskrat he had caught in a trap, who had but one leg, the other three having been chewed off during previous encounters with steel leg-hold traps. The muskrat was but another illustration of a supreme law: "Only courage does anywhere prolong life, whether of man or beast." Henry found no courage in the action of either his government or its military men in their imperial war upon Mexico. The American soldier was no better than the leg-hold trap, an unthinking killing machine set in motion by ruthless commanders. Henry was more like the muskrat, and would if necessary have sacrificed his own limbs to wage moral war against transgressors upon freedom, even when that freedom belonged to an unseen confrère.

Learning of his friend's incarceration, Emerson pronounced it "mean and skulking," and wrote in his journal: "The Abolitionists denounce the war and give much time to it, but they pay the tax . . . Don't run amuck against the world. As long as the state means you well, do not refuse your pistareen." Henry's defiance was characteristic of both his conviction and his capacity for communion. Enslaved African Americans and embattled Mexicans alike were felt by him to be close companions; any trap set for them was set for him as well. That solidarity was reflected in the fact that, a week after his night in jail, the antislavery society of Concord held its annual meeting on the doorstep of Henry's cabin, commemorating there the emancipation of slaves in West India. That very year, New London would become the scene of Joseph Cinqué and his fellow mutineer African slaves' trial; today, a reconstruction of the *Amistad* floats once again on the Thames, but it does so in the shadow of the Electric Boat nuclear submarine factory, and next to a patch of riverbank land designated for yet another war memorial—the Coast Guard Museum Association. Confronting such contemporary travesties of injustice, Henry would bust a gut if he trod this trail with me in the flesh, rather than ghostly spirit. Where had all the muskrats gone?

"What relevance does Henry David Thoreau have for us to-day?" journalists doing stories for Thoreau's bicentennial often asked me. It seems that there is no single American figure of more signal importance for this moment in American and world history. In the absence of an entire nation of scrappy muskrats, drawn from every little Norwich and New London across the land, we hide our shame and embarrassment and look for a single savior. We as a people collectively embody the exact *opposite* of what Henry was calling for when he spent the night in the Concord jail, or walked out to Walden Pond to live for two years. We have failed him so mightily that it feels like some tragic, epic myth of the sort that Henry himself might tell in *Walden*. Rather than be the radiant winged creature springing from a Connecticut farmer's handseled kitchen table, we risk becoming selfish seekers of luxury distracted by the very trivia that is the apotheosis of all that Henry warned about nearly two centuries ago.

To understatedly demonstrate his disdain for the materialist concerns of his petty bourgeois neighbors, Henry adopted the felicitous and familiar image of the cattle show, antebellum America's ubiquitous autumnal exhibition of agricultural splendor. "Cattle show" was his shorthand for petty amusements of the mob, and yet he had a local's fondness for the variegated display of men at the annual agricultural fair. In *A Week on the Concord and Merrimack Rivers*, he had painted a warmly sympathetic but unsentimental portrait of the farm folk at the fair, "come to see the sport, and have a hand in what is going,—to know 'what's the row,' if there is any; to be where some men are drunk, some horses race, some cockerels fight; anxious to be shaking props under a table, and above all to see the 'striped pig.'" Thoreau thought these men were the raw material of a fruitful future:

> Though there are many crooked and crabbed specimens of humanity among them, run all to thorn and rind, and crowded out of shape by adverse circumstances, like the third chestnut in the burr, so that you wonder to see some heads wear a whole hat, yet fear not that the race will fail or waver in them; like the crabs which grow in hedges, they furnish the stocks of sweet and thrifty fruits still. Thus is nature recruited from age to age, while the fair and palatable varieties die out, and have their period. This is that mankind.

Like Fanny Caulkins, Henry was an empathic phil-anthropist, given by nature to forgive small character failings and painfully aware of the same in his own imperfect character. Every man was welcome to the cattle show, "even a transcendentalist," Henry asserted.

But what in the world, pray tell, might Henry make of *our* cattle show? Concord's cattle show was but prelude; welcome, friends, to its inglorious apotheosis, its wholesale degeneration into full-blown imperial freak show. We may forgive the transcendentalist at the cattle show if he is rendered mute before such spectacle; it is not his job to call out the Emperor's New Clothes, but *ours*. *We* must don our muskrat suits and voice our outrage, crack our most cutting jokes, all while loving our neighbor. Can we do it?

℘

THE PRETTIEST STRETCH of road I had walked so far, Route 169 from Norwich north to Brooklyn, was in all the guidebooks as a must-do scenic drive: "Traverse one of the last unspoiled areas in the northeastern United States. This byway winds through history, passing colonial homesteads, churches, stone walls, meeting houses, and private schools as it connects classic New England towns. Views include maple and pine stands and glacially deposited rocks and boulders that lie strewn throughout fields." Some guidebook at some time since the birth of automobile tourism had christened this part of Connecticut the "Quiet Corner," and as I walked, I could not debate that designation. I was also enjoying the quiet of a total sabbatical from the news. What Henry said about the news 150 years ago holds true now more than ever: "I am sure that I never read any memorable news in a newspaper. If we read of one man robbed, or murdered, or killed by accident, or one house burned, or one vessel wrecked, or one steamboat blown up, or one cow run over on the Western Railroad, or one mad dog killed, or one lot of grasshoppers in the winter,—we need never read of another. One is enough. If you are acquainted with the principle, what do you care for a myriad instances and applications?"

When I passed through Canterbury, Connecticut, a wide vista of the lovely Quinebaug River as backdrop to the harmonious assemblage of church steeples and well-appointed chimneys made me feel for a moment as if I were one of Chaucer's pilgrims. But what a lonely pilgrim! If back along the Post Road I'd felt that there was too much company, trucks and cars filling my pilgrim's path, here in the Quiet Corner I felt the lack of society. It seemed that I should see other walkers out along this serene stretch of road, but none passed. It was rare to see a single pedestrian or even the occasional homeowner out in the yard. It was early spring, still too cold to be out gardening, and yet, where was everyone?

Just before reaching the village green in Brooklyn, home to the country's oldest agricultural fair, I came upon a large cemetery, and decided to bed down there for the night. Sleeping in cemeteries had been my lifelong habit; I had worked every summer in high school as a landscaper in our town's largest cemetery, and while traveling had come to regard all cemeteries as impromptu hostels offering the visitor both landscaped sanctuary and an open window into a town's past. Picking my way along the lichen-covered stone wall, I found a corner where there were no headstones, and the overhanging oaks from the adjacent forest had left an ample pile of dry leaves up against the wall, making a perfect bed.

The next morning, as I poked about the headstones, a man in a pickup truck came along and called through his open window: "Did you find Israel Putnam's grave? The bones are all gone now; wasn't much of him when they dug him up in 1888 to put in the new monument." The man, who had grown up on a chicken farm nearby, had come to the cemetery looking for a classmate who had recently passed away. "Israel Putnam was a born leader. He killed the last wolf in Connecticut, and when he heard about the Battles of Lexington and Concord, he dropped his plow to go join the army, and became a famous general. But like I said, he's not there now. He's buried up beneath the statue."

The man continued on, leaving me to circle back to the Revolutionary War hero's grave that I had overlooked. Engraved into the cover of a large crypt, an inscription proclaimed that Israel Putnam had been "ever attentive to the lives and happiness of his men." This generous memory filled me with melancholy, for somehow, on this gray day, I could feel nothing but my own lack of heroism, and the increasing sense that I had mapped out a fruitless pilgrimage that served no one but myself. I felt unfit to sing my own hero's song.

Returning to the road north, I immediately passed the fairgrounds, and recalled that I had gone there once, in 1981, when I had been living with my wife and five-year-old daughter, just over the state line, in Greene, Rhode Island. I had dim memories of cotton candy and fried dough, and a very strong memory of a red balloon. My daughter Jordan had spied a golden teddy bear with bright red overalls, hung upon the top row of a shooting gallery, and she dragged me over to win it for her. To do so, I would only need to pop one of the dozens of balloon targets with a dart. For $5 I got three tries; pop the balloon on your first throw, and take your pick from the top row.

Isn't it odd how, just before you do something you know you cannot do, you know you *can* do it; indeed, *you already have done it*—have leaped that brook, popped that single balloon, said the thing you could never say? That was the essence of my memory of that Brooklyn fairgrounds moment; I took a breath, aimed at the center of the red balloon, and, when it popped, casually pointed to the golden bear in red pantaloons. Jordan immediately called her new friend "Red Balloon."

When I was teaching history at a university, I once had a student who, before every exam, would write in large letters on the front page: BREATHE! Even the fit and ever confident Henry Thoreau and Israel Putnam, before they faced certain tasks, must have occasionally needed to mentally remind themselves to breathe, to pause just enough to steady their hand and mind. I do the same now, and write:

#9: BREATHE! into your fear and melancholy.

CHAPTER 10

The Respectable Folks: WHISPER!

WALKING—long, meditative walking—is a way to stop time, to enter eternity, shake off the present and past. When all is said and done, Henry's sojourn at Walden Pond aimed at exactly this: eternity. What a lovely discovery it is that one can arrive at the eternal by either taking up one's cross and walking, or by laying it down, and stopping. With so much latitude to reach Heaven, why is it that we so consistently arrive in Hell?

Or, shall I say, *make* Hell, for it surely is a human, not divine, creation. The problem of time is much bound up with our perennial self-generated fall. Since Henry's time, that problem has grown considerably more pressing; he wrestled with the railroad and telegraph, while we wear Apple Watches and set a dozen daily alarms on our cell phones.

Over what now is a pretty long lifetime as a professional historian, I've noticed a different but no less perplexing problem:

as our knowledge of the past grows, with finer and finer–grained portraits of the wider and wider spectrum of societies and cultures, and as our abilities to disseminate these portraits—via smart and sumptuously curated online exhibitions, podcasts, and galleries—grows, our collective wisdom diminishes. Awash in a tidal wave of digital images and text, the profession of academic history—and "lay" history as well—has succeeded in obliterating any meaning that history once held. History has largely become a tale told by a well-intentioned, eloquent, digital idiot, signifying nothing beyond its own self-reference. Despite periodic interruptions of professional cries for a "return to story," or the recent "rage for memoir," or any one of a dozen "Big History" fads and fashions, this once glorious arena of imparting august identity and noble aspirations to humanity is a tottering Tower of Babel.

I would sit down right now upon a stump with Henry, to see what this counter of tree rings and close student of Cotton Mather's *Magnalia Christi Americana* might say to stop me in my bitter blathering tracks. But here I will spare you, dear reader, for should I dive into *Walden* just now, and attempt to surface with all of Henry's insights about the domain of memory, and the practice of remembering, I would remain mired in the mud like Henry's lead plumb bob. He is, even in his concise Yankee mother wit, way too wide and deep to fathom in this chapter's brief pages, and I would have you make this swim yourself.

Autodidact that he was, Henry's histories are as idiosyncratic and original as his philosophy and natural history. But I think I have espied a limit to their wisdom. Take all of the keen and subtle historical insights in *A Week*, *Walden*, *Cape Cod*, *The Maine Woods*, not to mention the absolute originality of the history in his natural histories, and still, for a unique and priceless American prophet, they come up short as to the demands of our own time. I used to always say about Henry that he wholly fit my definition of a prophet—one who saw the future not because he had some clairvoyant gifts lacking in his contemporaries, but because he lived and breathed eternal verities. In *Expect Great Things*, I wrote that if the universal world turtle is to go on crawling toward the stars, we must regain sight of such eternal verities, very soon.

Out upon this road to Walden, I have become convinced that this recommitment to eternal verities (of the very sort that Henry so superbly achieved with *Walden*) is not enough. Time, dear reader, is speeding up, not just because of cell phones and smart cars and the World Wide Web and the Internet of Things. These are the mere shadow cast by a much more profound quickening, one whose nature remains as yet undefined and inchoate. If you have not lately felt it, ask around. By the time you abandon your inquiry, you will yourself find it to be true.

❧

WALKING INTO SOUTHBRIDGE, Massachusetts, it felt as if time—at least the recent decade of innovation and prosperity that is everywhere in evidence in my Brooklyn, New York, home or most of the villages on my route—had passed the little mill town by. On the main street, smack-dab in the center of town, stood a commercial block—built in Southbridge's heyday, no doubt—that was charred by fire. The roof was partially caved in. Clearly the ruin had stood this way for quite some time.

As is true of dozens of Massachusetts mill towns, Southbridge's situation on the Quinebaug River made it a prime site for gristmills and sawmills in the eighteenth century, and then textile mills in the nineteenth. By the 1930s, Polish, Greek, and Italian immigrants joined the Irish and French Canadian families who had come to work in the mills after the Civil War. One mill went from regional to world fame; the Wells family's American Optical Company ("AO" to locals) became the world's largest manufacturer of ophthalmic products, and at its height employed more than six thousand people. During World War II, AO workers were exempted from the draft, since they were manufacturing military components, including bombsights. There was even some work on the atomic bomb. By the early 1960s, Southbridge had a movie theater, an AM radio station (WESO), and an airport. New immigrants from Puerto Rico, Laos, and Vietnam began arriving in the 1970s and 1980s. Then, in 1984, American Optical shut down. The unattended burned-out store is just the kind of picture that ensured that the slogan "Make America Great Again" would resonate across the land.

There is a reason William Blake called mills "Satanic," and why "Mill Dam" for Henry symbolized not prosperity but a sort of creeping soul death. "Lives of quiet desperation" might manifest anywhere, but, when the human being wed himself too deeply to machines, he accelerated that decay. Glance into any coffee shop or now even a bar, and try not to think of Medusa turning those who gaze at her into stone. How is it that we have chosen that mesmerizing machine screen as our soul's close companion, when all about us are *real* souls, in desperate need of our loving attention? If we would put our hands upon the true "crank within," might we not put those infernal midget mills away for good?

The library had prepared a display of Thoreau's works and biographies on a table in the room where I was to speak, and this invited me to consider my own preparation. Just before arriving, I had found myself anxious at the prospect of another encounter where the rhyming riddle—contained in three poems Thoreau wrote that speak about his relationship to the elemental beings of nature—would go unsolved. In my journal I had written: "I hope today that *someone* will guess the answer to the riddle. If not, I think it is safe to say that:

"THE FAIRIES ARE FORGOTTEN."

My pessimistic state of expectation felt unfair and altogether a transgression against Henry's "expect great things" motto. I tried to think about what I might be doing to contribute to people's puzzlement at my "Who are the respectable folks?" question. Perhaps if I spoke more slowly, or repeated the verse?

I had forgotten that the respectable folk were crepuscular creatures, and the fluorescent lights of each room where I had performed were hardly conducive to drawing them near. Neither were the straight rows of chairs; I asked a staff member if I might dim the lights and rearrange the chairs in a circle. The first guests entered, a woman named Faith, along with her friend Sue. Another dozen people arrived, shook off their wet coats, and took a seat. Robert, a young man of about seventeen, told us he had read *Walden* recently and fallen in love with Thoreau. He was the first teenager to come to the *Huckleberry Party* since I had set up Broadway, and from just a few remarks, he was clearly a Huckleberry Captain—bright, inquisitive, keenly attuned to nature and history. Robert sat in the circle directly to my left; a woman named Rebecca sat to my right. I was in a playful mood, happy now that even if no one guessed the riddle, the respectable folks had given me an affirmation about the "book magic" book.

The circle seemed settled—time to begin. I left the circle, went to the back of the room, and entered again, singing Henry's favorite song—"Tom Bowling," an eighteenth century parlor ballad composed by Tom's younger brother about a favored young man who dies at sea:

Here, a sheer hulk, lies poor Tom Bowling
The darling of our crew
No more he'll hear the tempest howling
For death has broached him to.

I was sure that Henry had adopted the song as an anthem in memory of his beloved brother John, whom he had also lost way too soon. But the verses portraying Tom, or John, might as well have been written about Henry:

His form was of the manliest beauty
His heart was kind and soft.

Faithful below, Tom did his duty
But now he's gone aloft, but now he's gone aloft.

The song spoke of how Tom "never from his word departed," of how "his virtues were so rare," and of his many true-hearted friends.

After the song, I proposed the riddle, confessing that it was now the tenth day since I had begun, and no one had as yet come up with the answer to my question "Who are the 'respectable folk'?" I promised that—in the spirit of all good things in threes—I would give them three tries, since Henry had written three different poems about this enigmatic tribe.

The respectable folks,—
Where dwell they?
They whisper in the oaks,
And they sigh in the hay;
Summer and winter, night and day,
Out on the meadow, there dwell they.
They never die,
Nor snivel, nor cry,
Nor ask our pity
With a wet eye.
A sound estate they ever mend
To every asker readily lend;
To the ocean wealth,
To the meadow health,
To Time his length,
To the rocks strength,

To the stars light,
To the weary night,
To the busy day,
To the idle play;
And so their good cheer never ends,
For all are their debtors, and all their friends.

I exaggerated each accompanying gesture: whispering *whisper*; sighing *sigh*; miming *snivel* and *cry*; stretching my arms wide to show *time's length*, and clutching my clenched fists before me at *the rock, strength*. At the verse riddle's last word—*friends*—I paused longer than I usually did, closing my eyes and recalling my anxious journal expectation of earlier that day.

"Fairies," said Rebecca, in a calm, low voice, just as everyone in the circle turned to look toward the entrance, as three people came into the room. It was Margaret Morrissey, director of the library, along with a young couple named Chuck and Christine. Because of the momentary commotion, no one had heard Rebecca's answer! The circle now had thirteen people; I could go forward with the other two poems, giving the new audience members a chance to guess the riddle.

After asking Rebecca if she would keep her answer to herself, I launched into Henry's second poem, explaining that here Henry had called the respectable folk a "slender clan," "titmen" a "finer race":

Tell me ye wise ones if ye can
Whither and whence the race of man.

For I have seen his slender clan
Clinging to hoar hills with their feet,
Threading the forest for their meat.
Moss and lichens, bark and grain
They rake together with might and main
And they digest them with anxiety and pain.
. . . . .

They are the titmen of their race,
And hug the vales with mincing pace
Like Troglodytes, and fight with cranes.
. . . .

These elder brothers of our race,
By us unseen with larger pace
Walk o'er our heads, and live our lives,
Embody our desires and dreams,
Anticipate our hoped-for gleams.
. . . .

We hear their sounds and see their sights,
And we experience their delights.
But for the moment that we stand
Astonished on the Olympian land. . .

Rebecca had a smile on her face and in her eyes, but the rest of the circle wore frustrated frowns. "Nature?" proposed one tentative voice. "Trees?" another offered. I suggested that perhaps the third time would be the charm, and spoke out the third of Henry's poems, in which he called the respectable folk the "creature of a different destiny":

In concord, town of quiet name
And quiet fame as well,
Ive seen ye, sisters, on the mountain–side
When your green mantles fluttered in the wind
Ive seen your foot-prints on the lakes still shore
Lesser than man's, a more ethereal trace,
I have heard of ye as some far famed race,
Daughters of gods, whom I should one day meet,
I reverence your natures, so like mine
Yet strangely different, like but still unlike
Thou only stranger that has crossed my path,
Accept my hospitality; let me hear
The message which thou bring'st.
Made different from me,
Perchance thou'rt made to be
The creature of a different destiny.

In spite of all this descriptive detail, the circle was again mute. I tried teasing out some of the clues: "in concord" (the lowercase *c* allowing him to both give the location of his experience and his inner emotional state at the time) Henry had seen diminutive green-clad women on the mountainside, who left tiny footprints along the lakeshore. Like men, a "race," these "sisters" were also quite unlike humans, having a very different destiny. Like the respectable folks of the first poem, these sisters seemed unappreciated, giving of themselves but never receiving like courtesy from human beings. Henry has the perfect attitude toward them, the one that all authors have prescribed to the fairy world: an attitude of deference as well as reverence, not using their name, not asking anything from them, and indeed offering an attitude of true hospitality, and even concern that no one seems to take care of *them* while they so generously take care of us. Henry seems to know that he lives by their grace.

Still, this Southbridge circle of earnest and attentive listeners wrinkled their brows, looked upward left and right, turned and shrugged their shoulders at their neighbors, and gave up. I invited Rebecca to speak out her answer once again. A collective sigh and chuckle went up from the circle, and Margaret seemed happiest of all.

"Oh, yes, I grew up in Ireland with countless stories of the wee folk—of their antics and escapades. As children we thought nothing of being told that we must be very careful to respect the fairies, else they might come and clobber us in the night, or spoil the milk, or even steal our souls away for a time."

None of the other audience members chimed in with their own stories of the respectable folk, but clearly they had been witnessed, and welcomed, in this Massachusetts mill town, and perhaps one witness was enough.

Half a dozen people bought books, and I was just beginning to inscribe Rebecca's when I heard her say to another woman: "My brother wrote a book about Thoreau, I think." I lifted my pen and looked at her. "Who is your brother?" I asked.

"Lewis Hyde."

Instantly I saw in my mind's eye Lewis Hyde's signature on the bottom of a small piece of stationery with "Harvard University Department of English and American Literature and Language" on the letterhead. In 1988, having just read Lewis Hyde's *The Gift: Imagination and the Erotic Life of Property*, I wrote him a fan letter, and received a lovely note of gratitude in return. The note was stuck in the back of what must have been my third or fourth copy of the book; I seemed to have given away a copy every few years since I had first read it.

"I read your brother's edition of Thoreau's essays when I was writing *Expect Great Things*, but I never wrote to him as I had when I'd read *The Gift*. Will you please tell him thank you for those essays?"

Rebecca was shy, unpretentious, and spoke in soft, matter-of-fact tones. She seemed just the sort of person the respectable folks would seek out to whisper in her ear.

℘

WITHOUT DWELLING MUCH upon them, Henry in his journal from time to time would report on precognitive dreams that had come to him. While Margaret Fuller and others in the Concord circle were—like the Puritans of old—fairly obsessed with signs and auguries and omens, Henry took these glimpses of the future in stride, almost seeming to feel they were of a piece with his "demoniacal" desires. Intense personal desire, coupled with an acute imagination, seemed to be able to carry a person out of the present, to both past and future. During dreaming sleep, Henry knew that he could walk far beyond the far hills of Wachusett or even the Maine woods. He felt the heavenly hierarchies close around him, even within him. This communion with the angelic world formed the basis of his theory of dreams:

A part of me which has reposed in silence all day, goes abroad at night, like the owl, and has its day. At night we recline, and nestle, and in fold ourselves in our being. Each night I go home to rest. Each night I am gathered to my fathers. The soul departs out of the body, and sleeps in God, a divine slumber. As she withdraws herself, the limbs droop and the eyelids fall, and nature reclaims her clay again. Men have always regarded the night as ambrosial or divine. The air is peopled then—fairies come out.

Henry had not only built his Walden Pond temple by his diurnal haunting of the place, but by his nocturnal dream sojourns there. A month after coming to Walden, he recalled his first visit to the pond at age five: "That woodland vision for a long time made the drapery of my dreams. That sweet solitude my spirit seemed so early to require that I might have room to entertain my thronging guests, and that speaking silence that my ears might distinguish the significant sounds." It is not quite clear if he actually dreamed of the place *before* he visited it; given the intensity of his fidelity to the place, it seems very likely that it visited him before he visited it.

In my pilgrimage of life, I have often been visited by the wee "wise ones," and have been also visited by places and people and events before I visited them; I am pretty sure it is why these cryptic confessions in Henry's writings made a more distinct impression upon me than upon other biographers. In his most ecstatic, most inspired and inspiring moments, Henry always managed to whisper, to speak in hushed tones so as to please both the angels and the elementals. I would do the same, and say only that I speak of the respectable folks from a little distance, a distance that I pray will be pleasing to them.

#10: When you wish to honor the invisible, please WHISPER.

CHAPTER 11

A Track Repairer in the Orbit of the Earth: LOSE!

THOSE ENGINEERS AND SCOFFERS of the world who still repeat about Henry the silly hearsay critique about his mother baking him pies and doing his laundry could at least level the other nonsensical barrel at him: "What wilderness!? The Fitchburg Railroad skirted Walden Pond just a hundred yards from his cabin!" Yes, in fact, Henry says just that, in the "Sounds" chapter of *Walden*. "I usually go to the village along its causeway, and am, as it were, related to society by this link," crows this world-famous walker and happy hermit, who was even happier to avail himself of the railroad right-of-way as a shortcut into Concord Village. He reported that many who frequented the train took him to be a railroad employee; he turned this, his neighbors' error, to cosmically humble account: "I too would fain to be a track-repairer somewhere in the orbit of the earth."

Though Henry might make hay of the railroad's convenience, he was unabashed in calling out the havoc it wrought on human lives. "To make a railroad round the world available to all mankind is equivalent to grading the wide surface of the planet," he declared. "We do not ride upon the railroad; it rides upon us." Do not the computer and the "smart" phone ride upon us too?

$\mathcal{B}$

"I LONG AGO lost a hound, a bay horse, and a turtle dove, and am still on their trail," wrote Henry in *Walden*. "Many are the travelers I have spoken to concerning them, describing their tracks and what calls they answered to. I have met one or two who had heard the hound, and the tramp of the horse, and even seen the dove disappear behind a cloud, and they seemed as anxious to recover them as if they had lost them themselves." Losing plays a tremendous but much overlooked role in our personal destiny; especially here in America, we are addicted to winning.

Out on the road to Walden, walking long stretches of road uninterrupted by any discoveries or ecstasies, I often found myself calling into question my own casting of Henry as uniquely favored, as fortunate as his boyhood hero Fortunatus, whose magic hat and purse eased his way through life. Was this just wishful thinking on my part? Had I misread and then misrepresented Henry's entire enterprise? What about the failures, the not-so-great things, the outright tragedies in Henry's biography? Had I skipped over them just to satisfy my own appetite for easy blessings? Sometimes one expected great things and they did not come. Sometimes—often, in fact—one lost, not won.

Henry lost far more over his short life than a hound, a bay

horse, and a turtle dove. He lost his first and only romantic love, the lovely Ellen Sewall—to whom both he and his brother John proposed marriage—to her father's expectation of a more suitable suitor. He lost his beloved brother John when Henry was but twenty-four; this loss he felt so deeply that a week after John's death, he experienced all the symptoms of the painful lockjaw that John had endured after his razor-sliced finger had become infected. In the midst of this episode of "sympathetic" dying, Emerson's five-year-old son Waldo, to whom Henry was like a second father, contracted scarlet fever; three days later, he was dead. Seven years after John died, their sister Helen died—of consumption, the illness that would prematurely take Henry's life as well.

Henry's youthful ambitions to become America's bard, an ambition kindled and stewarded by his mentor Emerson, were frustrated at every turn, his idiosyncratic style and stubborn resistance to fashion ensuring that his essays and poems would be rejected for publication. When *A Week on the Concord and Merrimack Rivers* was published in 1849, the publisher insisted that Henry pay the cost of the book's production if it didn't sell; for years after it was mostly panned by shortsighted, opaque critics. Henry self-mockingly bragged that he was the owner of a library of nearly nine hundred volumes, over seven hundred of which he had written himself.

The deepest loss sustained by Henry in his brief life was the loss of his friendship with Ralph Waldo Emerson, whom he always called simply "my friend." Despite his appreciation of his eccentric protégé, Emerson faulted Henry for lacking ambition—the "captain of a huckleberry" dismissal—and for his too intimate intimacy with nature: "Very seductive are the first steps from the town to the woods, but the End is want & madness," Emerson warned. From his side, Henry was deeply wounded by the limits of his friend's capacity for intimacy with both himself and with God: "We do not believe in the same God. I am not thou—Thou art not I . . . Here I have been on what the world would call friendly terms with one fourteen years, have pleased my imagination sometimes with loving him—and yet our hate is stronger than our love." The quarrel between them echoed in some way the quarrel America had with itself over its own fate, a quarrel that is as yet very much unsettled. Where Henry put his faith firmly in himself as a "common man," Emerson, for all his fine words about democracy, never shared such faith, paying true democracy only lip service. While Emerson sought intellectual and spiritual treasure in the Old World, Henry dug deeper and deeper into this New World native land of his, convinced that the lode held there was as rich as anywhere upon Earth.

America, like Emerson, was a bit glib, liked to hear itself talk, and as a consequence frequently failed as a listener. The contrariness in Henry that so disturbed Emerson was Thoreau's first line of defense against succumbing to smug confidence in wan and wayward truths. If America as a nation practiced Henry's adage "A man must see, before he can say"— one I embraced and echoed in Chapter Two—it might more readily act with wisdom.

And so it was for this American, despite my love and respect for Henry's wisdom. I too am glib, like to hear myself talk, and always come up short as a listener, not just to my neighbors, students, and family, but to my own higher self. Gifted with the most extra-vagant blessings—that unwritten *Book Magic* only barely touches upon the prodigious presents the spiritual world has showered upon me, at the mere whisper of my desire—I have repeatedly squandered them, putting them to mundane rather than sublime employment. I have not sufficiently stored up treasures in Heaven, but have settled over and over for the ephemeral satisfactions of the physical senses.

Henry could "call in" from the world rare plants, arrowheads, music boxes. The consistency with which he was confronted with the plain fact of his *daimonological* power of desire over just these three things perplexed him his whole life long. Along with rare plants and arrowheads, I have called in treasures as diverse as rattlesnake skins, antique coins, magic hats, and a brand-new dobro—a steel resonator guitar. The dobro took only seventeen hours to show up for me after I blurted out repeatedly that I wanted one. Clearly, the reason that I fell in love with Lewis Hyde's *The Gift* was the same reason I fell in love with Henry: they celebrated the cosmos's cornucopian abundance. Heaven was here, all around us, if we just opened to that reality. To the degree that we but aligned with our own destiny, we could have whatever we wanted.

❦

I MAY EVEN have been thinking these prodigal thoughts on that penultimate day of my pilgrimage, somewhere between Worcester and Concord, when I ducked out of the cold rain into a convenience store. As I entered, there was a severely underdressed man at the counter buying cigarettes. The cashier, an Indian man with a broad smile and soft eyes, spoke gently to his customer, but the customer barely acknowledged the courtesy, turned, and was out the door. A moment later a woman entered, went straight to the back of the store, and slid open one of the reach-ins to pull out a gallon of milk. At the counter, she pointed at one of the lottery ticket displays, and muttered something about her lack of luck as the cashier slid a bunch of tickets across the glass toward her open palm. Before she stepped away, in came a little old man ranting what sounded like a litany of complaints aimed at the Indian man, all said Popeye-fashion, under the breath, but loudly and angrily. He pushed past the lady, grabbed a Bic lighter from the counter display, and slapped it onto the glass, then threw a pair of crumpled dollar bills down, and walked out.

Now that the rush had ended, I asked the man if he had any M&M's. Digging into my "Nuts & Chocolate" trail mix that morning, I had found that they had forgotten the chocolate, and my mouth was crying out for some third texture to break the monotony of raisins and peanuts. He motioned just behind me, and I reached for the jumbo bag of peanut butter M&M's. I was a dollar short, and was about to put them back and pick out a smaller bag, when the man said: "Oh, that's all right. Keep these. No problem."

"Do you know that all my life, every day, I am hoping that someone will give me something for nothing, and it so rarely happens, but here you—a total stranger—have done just that? What is your name?"

"Affie—short for Aftab."

Another woman came in, for cigarettes, and then bought an instant lottery ticket. After quickly scratching at it, she dropped it back onto the counter.

"No good?" Affie asked her, but she didn't respond. "Want I throw it? I can throw it."

Still no reply from the woman, who was in a kind of daze.

"Garbage? No good?"

The woman finally came to. "No, no good," she managed, and Affie tossed the ticket in the trash. There was an awkward silence for what seemed a very long time, and then the woman picked up her cigarettes, turned, and went out the door.

"How much gaming and gambling is there back in India?" I asked Affie.

"No. Nothing, not in the open, in plain sight!" Affie laughed. "We don't have lottery over there like that. People make their own things, not out in open."

"Isn't it sick, Affie? Get rich quick! This is the civic religion of America."

"It's not just America, I don't believe," he countered. "It's personal, everybody have their own method. I don't care about money; probably that's why I don't have it. It's important, but it's just not everything, to me. It's good to have it, but it's not, like, to die for. Humanity is first, any other thing is second."

Affie tells me the whole story of how he has come to be in the store. Twenty years ago he left Cambridge, England, to come out here to help his brother, who had bought the store, but had to return to India because their father was sick. Affie was the youngest of nine children; his brother, the eldest, was expected to return. But the woman who sold the store had cheated Affie's brother, it was very complicated, and there were still debts, and so it was that two decades had passed, and here he was, a bright, sweet, generous man, faithfully working seven days a week. Was there no one else who might help? His wife? No, he would not let her work in here.

Another customer came in. More lottery tickets and cigarettes. No beer, because they had lost their license to sell alcohol. ("I didn't know. I should have known" Affie said mildly, with not one bit of bitterness.)

"Yes, get everything you need today," I said to this woman. "Tomorrow you will find a sign—GONE FISHIN'—and Affie is going to go fishing with me, his first day off in twenty years."

The woman, uncomfortable with my familiarity, shuffled out, and Affie smiled.

℘

AMERICA HAS NEVER learned the sacred lesson of surrender. "I left the woods for as good a reason as I went there," said Henry after two years in his woodland temple. Henry had every reason to be able to tell Emerson and Bronson Alcott and Margaret Fuller and even George Melvin the trapper: *It's been a good run. I left before the moss grew on me.*

℘

ALL MY LIFE, I have prided myself on finding things—stories, treasures, secrets. It is a conceit that colors my image of Henry

Thoreau, and of my relation to him as biographer as well as student and friend. For all his heroic martial bluster, for all his abilities as discoverer of mysteries large and small, Henry Thoreau knew well the alchemy of loss, of surrender. Coming ever closer to Thoreau's cabin, I could not help feeling that this might be the true meaning of my pilgrimage, that it demanded surrender rather than discovery.

#11: SURRENDER that which no longer serves you.

CHAPTER 12

TRANSCEND!

Speaking with hundreds of people along the road to Walden, I often found people—including well-read individuals, who had even read *Walden*—fumbling to define "transcendentalism." "They were a group of thinkers in Concord, Massachusetts, who wanted to transcend, to get to another world." That innocent tautology comes about closest to the reigning definition living out there on the road to Walden, and thus in America in 2017, I would say.

Henry was hardly afraid to claim the identity. When the American Association for the Advancement of Science sent him a membership questionnaire, he returned it, but to his journal he confided that he could never explain to the AAAS the branch of science that occupied him, since they "do not believe in a science which deals with a higher law." "The fact is," he admitted, "I am a mystic, a transcendentalist, and a natural philosopher to boot." On second thought, he decided that the best way

to inform the august scientific body that they would not understand him was to tell them "at once that I was a transcendentalist."

Yes, indeed, Henry was all transcendentalist, all the time,
though his contemporaries were as befuddled by him as we
seem to be. He got the habit early and hard. As young children,
Henry and his older brother John slept in a trundle bed in their
parents' room, and while John would go to sleep at once, Henry
would often lie awake for a long time, looking up at the stars
through the window. When his mother once asked him why he
didn't go to sleep, he replied, "Mother, I have been looking
through the stars to see if I couldn't see God behind them." The
boy had a precocious gift for expansiveness, as keen an eye for
the heavens as for huckleberries. That, dear reader, is why I
christened this pair of walkers—myself and my spectral companion Henry—Captains of a Huckleberry Party.

I might as well have said "Pinxter Flower Party." One May,
Henry's sister Sophia brought home a single blossom of the *Azalea nudiflora*, or pinxter flower, from Mrs. Brooks, a neighbor.
Learning from Mrs. Brooks that George Melvin had given the
plant to her son, he found the son at work, only to discover that
he didn't know where Melvin had gotten it. Hearing that someone had seen the shrub at Captain Jarvis's, Henry went there
and found some in the house, but they had gotten theirs from
Melvin and didn't know from where he had gotten it. At Sted-
man Buttrick's he found a young man who said that there was
only one bush in the area and its location was a secret. Henry
went on to Melvin's house, expecting not to find him in, but

when he arrived, there sat Melvin, bareheaded in the shade by the back door, a large pail full of the elusive azaleas beside him.

Melvin "dilly-dallied" a bit, calling to his neighbor to ask if he knew where that "red honeysuckle" grew. "This was to prolong the time and make the most of his secret," Henry accused. Then he recalled running into Melvin up the Assabet River a few weeks previously when he had gone to collect a mustard in flower. Melvin had appeared out of the woods, and, seeing Henry's flower, had commented that it was "not so handsome as the honeysuckle." Now he realized that Melvin's "honeysuckle" was the pinxter flower, and Henry told Melvin:

> He had better tell me where it was; I was a botanist and ought to know . . . I told him he'd better tell me and have the glory of it, for I should surely find it if he didn't. I'd got a clue to it, and shouldn't give it up. I should go over the river for it . . . I could smell it a good way, you know. He thought I could smell it half a mile, and he wondered that I hadn't stumbled on it . . .

Getting into his boat with his dog, Melvin took Henry to the coveted bush, and showed him how close Ellery Channing had once passed by it while it was in flower. Melvin had found it ten years before, and went to it every year, thinking it "the handsomest flower that grows." This episode of the pinxter flower suggests the degree to which Concord's mother wit about the local landscape was dispersed throughout the entire community. Although Henry possessed special knowledge, he never ceased appealing to others to share what they knew with him.

Once he finally arrived at the prize shrub, Henry approached it with the same exactness as he did any other phenomenon, and gives in his journal a thorough description, commenting particularly on a characteristic—its clamminess—not noted in his botanical manuals. But the careful taxonomic examination did not obscure for Thoreau the fact that the quest for *Azalea nudiflora* was mythic—one might say "transcendental"—as much as scientific:

Some incidents in my life have seemed far more allegorical than actual; they were so significant that they plainly served no other use. That is, I have been more impressed by their allegorical significance and fitness; they have been like myths or passages in a myth, rather than mere incidents or history which have to wait to become significant. Quite in harmony with my subjective philosophy. This, for instance: that when I thought I knew the flowers so well, the beautiful azalea or pinxter-flower should be shown me by the hunter who found it. Such facts are lifted quite above the level of the actual. They are all just such events as my imagination prepares me for, no matter how incredible. Perfectly in keeping with my life and characteristic. Ever and anon something will occur which my philosophy has not dreamed of. The limits of the actual are set some thoughts further off. That which had seemed a rigid wall of vast thickness unexpectedly proves a thin and undulating drapery. The boundaries of the actual are more fixed and rigid than the elasticity of our imaginations. The fact that a rare and beautiful flower which we never saw, perhaps never heard [of], for which therefore there was no place in our thoughts, may at length be found in our immediate neighborhood, is very suggestive.

The pinxter flower afforded Henry a glimpse of the mythic condition of his own life. The fact so striking to him—that such a rare plant should be found so close at hand—would have been exceptional in someone else's experience, but was unexceptional in his own. It was, rather, "perfectly in keeping with my life and characteristic." Yet another level of allegory escaped Henry's notice, for *pinxter* is the Dutch term for Whitsuntide, or Pentecost, when the newly baptized wear white robes signifying their exalted state. Named to commemorate its blossoming time about seven weeks after Easter Sunday, it was a fit plant to elicit such passion from Henry, given his obsession this season with the vernal phenology of local plants. Beyond this, though, the pinxter flower was emblematic of a kind of personal Pentecost for Henry; he could now, after his year of observation, speak in nature's own tongue, baptizing others not yet anointed with such grace.

ᘒ

SATURDAY, APRIL 1—April Fool's Day—it snowed about six inches on the road to Walden. Indeed, the snow was so thick and wet that the director of the Thoreau Farm, where I was meant to deliver my last performance of *Captain of a Huckleberry Party* in the room below the room where Henry was born, called me to say that she didn't think she would be able to get out of her driveway to come meet me. If worse came to worst, she said, she could tell me where the key was hidden, and I could let myself in. Certainly none of the guests who had promised to come—a *Boston Globe* reporter; John Kaag, who had reviewed *Expect Great Things* for the *New York Times*; my aunt and uncle who lived about forty-five minutes away in Peterborough, New Hampshire; and my cousin Bill, who had originally planned to walk with me on the Old Marlborough Road into Concord—would be likely to make it, given the weather.

It was far too dangerous to walk the sixteen miles that I had ahead of me, and so I decided to visit Nagog Pond in Acton, the next town north of Concord, to take a safe and soggy walk around its perimeter. Henry had had some strange experiences there, as had many others, for generation after generation since its shores served as America's first place of confinement for native peoples. I felt strong despite the wet snow, as if I might beckon there the benevolent respectable folks to heal and redeem any dark deeds of the past. It seemed just the sort of activity that Henry practiced every day of his brief life, and I felt honored to walk in his foolish footsteps there on an unseasonably inclement April Fool's Day. Oddly enough, but not so very oddly at all, almost at the end of my walk, I heard a series of explosions—and then realized these were the very same "Moodus Noises" that Thoreau had heard when he walked here, and that were said by the locals to be the angry spirits of the dead Wampanoag warriors buried close by the pond.

Even the deer were ducking the weather, so I found myself entirely alone on the walk, in a place that Henry had indeed walked, but still, it was not Walden Pond. I ended up a bit lost, and finally came out at a dead end of a little suburban development. Just as I emerged from a grove of white pine heavy with wet snow, a man approached, walking his dog.

"Did you hear those explosions?" I asked.

"All my life, and I've lived"—here he paused to point to a farmhouse directly behind him—"around this pond for seventy-two years. They say they're spirits. Could be, you know."

I felt close to Henry at this moment, certain that the sounds were caused by beings beyond our ken. It is a "fool's errand" to attend to the world's mysteries, to search for the laws underlying life's surfaces. It is, in a word, transcendentalism. As fool, as Captain of a Huckleberry Party, Henry Thoreau embodied and increased the fool's way in a manner that rings down through time to give us all confidence and delight in our own tom-foolishness.

What happens when enough of us become fools? Society transforms, transcends. Can we, dear friends, meet each other in the way that Thoreau and Emerson could not? And can we meet those beings who befuddled—even as they befriended—Henry, those elemental beings of Nature by whose magical grace we live?

Awake to our own souls and to the World Soul, we shall fitly fulfill the legacy that Henry left us. Speaking, dancing, creating, sensing, sympathizing, befriending, burning, breathing, whispering, surrendering, we shall:

#12: TRANSCEND the Times, as all Fools do.

12 Steps on
the Transcendental Trail

#1: AWAKE! And know that you have slept with Angels.

#2: SPEAK, always striving to know more than you say.

#3: Learn to DANCE, else the Angels won't know what to do with you.

#4: Become a Vortex—CREATE!

#5: SENSE your way toward the extrasensory.

#6: SYMPATHIZE yourself into the Creation and you shall become the bait for miracles.

#7: To make your World, BEFRIEND Heaven.

#8: Let the Fires within and without BURN away the inessential.

#9: BREATHE! into your fear and melancholy.

#10: When you wish to honor the invisible, please WHISPER.

#11: SURRENDER that which no longer serves you.

#12: TRANSCEND the Times, as all Fools do.

About the Author

Historian, naturalist, and troubadour **Kevin Dann** is the acclaimed author of *Expect Great Things: The Life and Search of Henry David Thoreau*, and books including *Across the Great Border Fault: The Naturalist Myth in America* and *Lewis Creek Lost and Found*. He received his PhD from Rutgers University in American history and environmental history. Dann has taught at Rutgers, the University of Vermont, and the State University of New York.

Come walk with Dr. Dann!
See http://drdann.com/about/walks